MOVIE ★ ICONS

BRANDO

EDITOR
PAUL DUNCAN

TEXT
F. X. FEENEY

PHOTOS
THE KOBAL COLLECTION

TASCHEN

HONG KONG KÖLN LONDON LOS ANGELES MADRID PARIS TOKYO

CONTENTS

1

MARLON BRANDO: HIS ANIMAL SELF

BY F. X. FEENEY

MARLON BRANDO: DAS TIER IM MANN

MARLON BRANDO : LA BÊTE HUMAINE

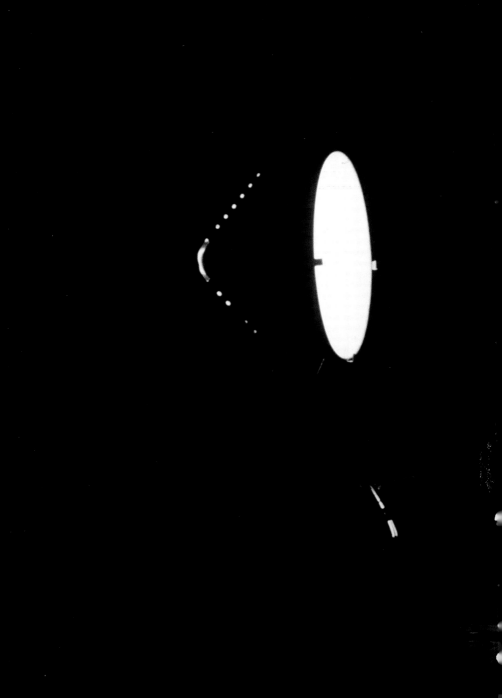

MARLON BRANDO: HIS ANIMAL SELF

by F. X. Feeney

"If I hadn't been an actor," Marlon Brando once wrote, "I'd have become a con man and wound up in jail. Or I might have gone crazy." Take him at his word. Too many complain that Brando, the greatest actor of his generation, wasted his life in futile rebellions and left far too few masterworks in his wake, especially when measured against his divinely-scaled potential. Measure him instead against his sincere confession of criminal and even insane potential, and we can be grateful for the little we do have. The actor who starred so unforgettably in *A Streetcar Named Desire*, *Viva Zapata!*, *On the Waterfront*, *The Godfather* and *Last Tango in Paris* certainly owes no apologies to posterity.

Judged purely in terms of talent and physicality, he had it all. Through his 20s and 30s, Brando was blessed with the body and beauty of an Achilles. He also enjoyed no small share of the great warrior's courage, or flashing temper – though these gifts were matched, and here comes the wounded heel, by a prideful, destructive moodiness. Few talents could sulk in their tents with greater drama or determination. Director Elia Kazan, who more or less discovered Brando, and nurtured him through his first two triumphs, *A Streetcar Named Desire* and *Viva Zapata!*, was reduced to pleading with the actor to star in what ultimately became their Oscar-winning third smash together, *On the Waterfront*. At separate times, both Sam Peckinpah and Stanley Kubrick hoped to direct *One-Eyed Jacks* – and each were spun in futile circles until Brando decided to direct it himself. Later in life, only the promise of paychecks written in multi-millions could bring the actor to the table. This explains why so many of his later films are comparatively beneath his gifts. Yet, even in these cases, he routinely tested the integrity of his courtiers by making deliberately weird and outrageous demands. Brando told director Richard Donner that he would only play the role of the father in *Superman* if he could do so dressed as

MARLON BRANDO (1951)
A skeptical eye cocked at Hollywood, despite the glamour. / Trotz des Glamours sieht er Hollywood mit einem skeptischen Auge. / Un œil sceptique jeté sur Hollywood en dépit du glamour.

"To grasp the full significance of life is the actor's duty, to interpret it is his problem, and to express it his dedication."
Marlon Brando

a giant green doughnut, or be a godlike voiceover, speaking from within a glowing suitcase. It was only after Donner flatly refused these proposals that Brando became respectful. This was a dance he forced many directors to do.

Genius was in his genes. His mother Dot Pennebaker ran a respected theater group in Nebraska and was locally renowned as an exceptional performer. Prior to her son and her daughter Jocelyn Brando, both of whose early stage careers she actively promoted, Dot was instrumental in launching a handsome but shy Omaha neighbor she had coaxed to try acting – Henry Fonda. Brando's rancher father, Marlon senior, was by contrast a physically powerful, violent, two-fisted drinker and "man's man." His canny business sense kept the family in comfortable style through the Depression era, but his love-hate fury at his wife's artistic pursuits (often badly complicated by her own drinking problem) put him on a lifelong collision course with his highly emotional son, whom he verbally abused throughout his adolescence. The two battled until well after the boy was full grown. Listen closely to the monologues Brando improvised in *Last Tango in Paris*, and the confession of his early sufferings could not be more explicit, or detailed. Even his published autobiography pales by comparison. Self-destructive beauty, a domineering nature, violent magnetism – the man the boy became is such a lucid vessel of the storms and torments which drove both his parents that it is small wonder so little of his life was devoted to being 'a great actor,' while so much of it was spent toying with 'lives not lived,' simply searching for himself.

His iconic power onscreen is that he is so unpredictable. Brando projects the unselfish menace of a jungle animal hunting for a thing he can't name. Whether he roughly seizes a woman, only to hold her with dreamy tenderness, or suddenly attacks another man, only to draw him into a deeper complicity in the next breath, these impulses come from such a depths as to be startling, no matter how much you might anticipate them, in film after film. James Baldwin wrote that we ask people onstage to act, but ask people on film to be. "To be or not to be," Hamlet's great question, is one Brando never needs to ask aloud – he embodies it, instant by fascinating instant.

MARLON BRANDO: DAS TIER IM MANN

von F. X. Feeney

„Wenn ich kein Schauspieler gewesen wäre", schrieb Marlon Brando einmal, „dann wäre ich Betrüger geworden und im Gefängnis gelandet. Oder ich wäre durchgedreht." Man darf ihn beim Wort nehmen. Zu viele klagen, dass Brando, der größte Schauspieler seiner Generation, das Leben mit sinnloser Aufsässigkeit verschwendet und viel zu wenige Meisterwerke hinterlassen habe - insbesondere, wenn man ihn an seinem schauspielerischen Potential misst, das geradezu göttliche Dimensionen hatte. Misst man ihn hingegen an seinem aufrichtig gestandenen Potential zur Kriminalität oder gar zur Geisteskrankheit, dann können wir uns durchaus glücklich schätzen über das Wenige, das wir von ihm besitzen. Ein Darsteller, der seine Hauptrollen in *Endstation Sehnsucht*, *Viva Zapata!*, *Die Faust im Nacken*, *Der Pate* und *Der letzte Tango in Paris* so unvergesslich spielte, muss sich vor seiner Nachwelt wahrlich nicht schämen.

Wenn man ihn nur nach Talent und Körperbau beurteilt, dann besaß er alles. In seinen Zwanzigern und Dreißigern war Brando mit dem Körper und dem Aussehen eines Achilles gesegnet. Wie jener große Krieger besaß auch er ein ordentliches Maß an Mut und Temperament, doch ging mit diesen Gaben - und hier kommt die verwundbare Ferse - eine ebenso stolze wie zerstörerische Launenhaftigkeit einher. Kaum ein Schauspieler konnte ihm in Sachen Dramatik und Entschlossenheit das Wasser reichen, wenn es ums Schmollen ging. Selbst Regisseur Elia Kazan, der Brando mehr oder weniger entdeckt und ihn mit seinen beiden ersten Triumphen, *Endstation Sehnsucht* und *Viva Zapata!*, zum Star gemacht hatte, musste betteln und flehen, damit Brando die Rolle in *Die Faust im Nacken* annahm, dem dritten „Oscar"-prämierten Kassenerfolg der beiden. Zu bestimmten Zeiten hofften sowohl Sam Peckinpah als auch Stanley Kubrick darauf, bei *Der Besessene* Regie führen zu dürfen – und beide ließ Brando monatelang in der Luft hängen, bis er das Ruder schließlich selbst in die Hand nahm. Später konnte ihn dann nur noch die Aussicht auf Millionengagen überhaupt an den Verhandlungstisch bringen. Diese Tatsache erklärt auch, warum viele seiner späteren Filme so weit unter seiner Begabung lagen. Aber selbst in diesen Fällen stellte er die Integrität seiner „Freier"

„Die Pflicht des Schauspielers ist es, die gesamte Bedeutung des Lebens zu erfassen, sein Problem, sie zu deuten, und seine Aufgabe, sie auszudrücken."
Marlon Brando

ON THE SET OF 'FROM HERE TO ETERNITY' (1953)
With rival, friend, and fellow passion artist Montgomery Clift. / Mit seinem Rivalen und Freund Montgomery Clift, der ebenfalls ein leidenschaftlicher Künstler war. / Avec son rival et néanmoins ami Montgomery Clift, autre artiste passionné.

regelmäßig auf die Probe, indem er absichtlich völlig absurde und absonderliche Forderungen stellte. Brando erklärte Regisseur Richard Donner ursprünglich, dass er die Rolle des Vaters in *Superman* nur als grüner Riesendonut verkleidet oder als gottähnliche Stimme spielen werde, die aus einem leuchtenden Koffer spricht. Erst nachdem Donner diese Ideen mit aller Entschiedenheit abgelehnt hatte, zollte Brando seinem Gegenüber Respekt. Solche Spielchen spielte er mit vielen Regisseuren.

Das Genie war ihm in die Wiege gelegt worden. Seine Mutter, Dorothy „Dot" Pennebaker, leitete eine angesehene Theatergruppe in Nebraska und galt dort als außergewöhnliche Schauspielerin. Schon bevor sie die frühe Theaterkarriere ihres Sohnes und ihrer Tochter Jocelyn Brando nachdrücklich förderte, hatte Dot einen gutaussehenden, aber schüchternen Nachbarn aus Omaha ermutigt, es doch einmal mit der Schauspielerei zu versuchen, und ihn anschließend unterstützt: Henry Fonda. Brandos Vater hingegen, Marlon senior, besaß eine Ranch und war ein kräftig gebauter, rauflustiger, gewalttätiger Trinker und Macho, doch dank seiner Sparsamkeit und seines Geschäftssinns ging es der Familie immerhin auch während der Wirtschaftskrise noch recht gut. Allerdings hatte er wenig Verständnis für die künstlerische Ader seiner Frau, die im Übrigen selbst mit Alkoholproblemen zu kämpfen hatte – was das Verhältnis nicht einfacher machte. Dadurch war ein lebenslanger Konflikt mit seinem hochgradig emotionalen Sohn, den er in seiner Jugend häufig beschimpfte, bereits vorprogrammiert. Diese Auseinandersetzungen hielten noch lange an, als der Junge längst erwachsen geworden war. Wenn man bei

ON THE SET OF 'EAST OF EDEN' (1955)
Elia Kazan (left) discovered him. James Dean (feigning indifference, right) worshipped him. / Elia Kazan (links) entdeckte ihn. James Dean (Gleichgültigkeit mimend, rechts) verehrte ihn. / Découvert par Elia Kazan (à gauche), Brando est adulé par James Dean (à droite, feignant l'indifférence).

den Monologen, die Brando in *Der letzte Tango in Paris* improvisierte, genau hinhört, könnte das Geständnis seines Leidensweges kaum deutlicher oder detaillierter ausfallen. Dagegen verblasst selbst seine veröffentlichte Autobiografie.

MARILYN MONROE & MARLON BRANDO (1954)
The two enjoyed a long, easygoing love affair until her death. / Die beiden verband eine lange, unbeschwerte Liebesbeziehung bis zu Marilyns Tod. / Les deux stars auront une liaison bon enfant jusqu'à la mort de Marilyn.

Selbstzerstörerisch gutes Aussehen, ein herrisches Wesen, brutale Anziehungskraft - der Mann, zu dem der Junge heranwuchs, vereinigte in solch starkem Maße das aufgewühlte Innenleben beider Elternteile, dass es kaum wundert, wenn er nur einen kleinen Teil seines Lebens der Aufgabe widmete, ein „großer Schauspieler" zu sein - und einen so großen Teil der reinen Selbstfindung.

Seine ikonenhafte Ausstrahlung auf der Leinwand rührt von seinem unberechenbaren Wesen her. Brando vermittelt die unwillkürliche Bedrohlichkeit eines wilden Tieres, das nach etwas jagt, das es selbst nicht wirklich benennen kann. Ob er eine Frau unsanft packt, um sie anschließend mit träumerischer Zärtlichkeit zu halten, oder plötzlich einen anderen Mann angreift, um ihn im nächsten Atemzug in eine tiefere Komplizenschaft zu ziehen - diese Impulse kommen aus solcher Tiefe, dass sie in jedem Film aufs Neue überraschen, auch wenn man sie kommen sieht. James Baldwin schrieb, dass wir von Menschen auf der Bühne erwarten, dass sie *spielen*, während wir von Menschen im Film erwarten, dass sie *sind*. „Sein oder nicht sein", Hamlets große Frage, musste sich Brando nie laut stellen - er verkörpert sie in jedem faszinierenden Augenblick.

MARLON BRANDO : LA BÊTE HUMAINE

F. X. Feeney

« Si je n'avais pas été acteur, a écrit un jour Marlon Brando, j'aurais été escroc et j'aurais fini en prison. Ou alors je serais peut-être devenu fou. » Vous pouvez le croire. Nombreux sont ceux qui déplorent que Brando, le plus grand acteur de sa génération, ait gâché sa vie dans de futiles rebellions et ait laissé dans son sillage bien trop peu de chefs-d'œuvre au regard de son prodigieux potentiel. Mais si l'on songe, comme il le confesse sincèrement, qu'il aurait pu sombrer dans la délinquance ou même dans la folie, on ne peut qu'être reconnaissant du peu qu'il nous a donné. L'acteur qui a laissé une empreinte si indélébile dans *Un tramway nommé désir*, *Viva Zapata!*, *Sur les quais*, *Le Parrain* et *Le Dernier Tango à Paris* ne doit certainement aucune excuse à la postérité.

Si l'on s'en réfère uniquement au talent et au physique, il avait tout. Jusqu'à la quarantaine, Brando est doué du corps et de la beauté d'un dieu grec. D'un héros antique, il possède également le courage et le tempérament fougueux, même si ces qualités s'accompagnent, et c'est là son talon d'Achille, d'un caractère lunatique, orgueilleux et destructeur. Peu de stars sont capables de bouder sous leur tente avec autant de grandiloquence et de détermination. Le réalisateur Elia Kazan, qui a plus ou moins découvert Brando et l'a accompagné pendant ses deux premiers triomphes, *Un tramway nommé désir* et *Viva Zapata!*, en est réduit à le supplier de figurer dans ce qui sera leur troisième grand succès couronné d'oscars, *Sur les quais*. Sam Peckinpah et Stanley Kubrick espéreront chacun à leur tour mettre en scène *La Vengeance aux deux visages* et tourneront en rond jusqu'à ce Brando décide de le réaliser lui-même. Par la suite, seule la promesse de cachets libellés en millions pourront amener l'acteur à la table des négociations. Ceci explique que bon nombre des films tournés à la fin de sa carrière ne soient pas à la hauteur de son talent. Et pourtant, il ne cesse de tester l'intégrité de ses courtisans par des exigences délibérément farfelues et outrancières. C'est ainsi qu'il déclare au réalisateur Richard Donner qu'il n'acceptera de jouer le rôle du père dans *Superman* que s'il apparaît sous les traits d'un énorme beignet vert ou d'une voix sépulcrale sortant d'une valise incandescente. Ce n'est qu'après avoir essuyé un refus sans appel qu'il daigne

MARLON BRANDO (1950)
All pulse, pure energy. What better musical instrument for Brando than bongos? / Alles Pulsschlag und ungebändigte Energie – welches Musikinstrument hätte besser zu Brando gepasst als Bongos? / Quel meilleur instrument que le bongo pour cet homme tout en pulsions et en énergie brute ?

« Saisir tout le sens de la vie est le devoir de l'acteur, l'interpréter est son problème, l'exprimer est sa raison d'être. »
Marlon Brando

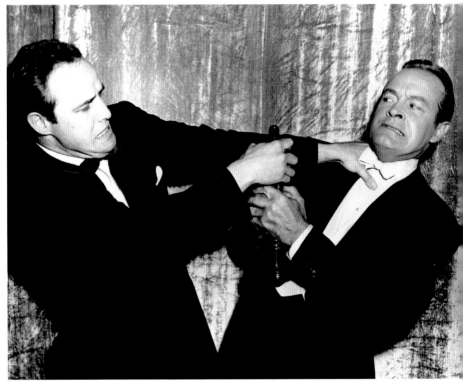

THE ACADEMY AWARDS (1954)
Clowning with Bob Hope over his Oscar for 'On the Waterfront.' / Als er seinen Oscar für *Die Faust im Nacken* entgegennimmt, spaßt er mit Moderator Bob Hope. / Faisant mine de se battre avec Bob Hope pour l'oscar de *Sur les quais.*

se montrer respectueux. Bien d'autres metteurs en scène seront contraints de jouer ce petit jeu.

Brando a le génie dans le sang. Sa mère, Dot Pennebaker, dirige une honorable troupe de théâtre dans le Nebraska et est réputée à l'échelle locale pour son exceptionnel talent d'actrice. Avant de promouvoir activement la carrière théâtrale de son fils et de sa fille Jocelyn Brando, Dot contribue à lancer un beau jeune homme timide qu'elle pousse sur les planches : Henry Fonda. À l'inverse, le père de Brando, Marlon senior, est un homme viril, violent et gros buveur. Son sens des affaires assure à la famille un train de vie confortable pendant la crise de 1929, mais ses réactions d'amour et de haine vis-à-vis des ambitions artistiques de sa femme (souvent aggravées par le penchant de cette dernière pour la boisson) instaurent un conflit permanent avec son fils, garçon émotif qu'il agressera verbalement tout au long de son adolescence. Ce conflit se poursuivra bien après l'entrée du jeune homme dans l'âge adulte. Écoutez attentivement les monologues improvisés par Brando dans *Le Dernier Tango à Paris*, et vous verrez que la confession de ses souffrances de jeunesse ne pourrait être plus explicite ni plus détaillée. Même son autobiographie fait pâle figure à côté.

21

Une beauté autodestructrice, une nature dominatrice, un violent magnétisme : l'homme qu'il est devenu porte si clairement la marque des tempêtes et des tourments qui ont agité ses parents qu'il n'est guère étonnant qu'il ait consacré si peu de sa vie à être « un grand acteur » et passé tant de temps à rêver « aux vies qu'il n'a pas vécues », tout simplement à la recherche de lui-même.

Sa légendaire présence à l'écran découle de son tempérament imprévisible. Brando projette la menace désintéressée d'une bête sauvage traquant une proie qu'elle ne peut nommer. Qu'il empoigne brutalement une femme avant de la serrer avec une tendresse rêveuse ou qu'il attaque soudain un autre homme pour l'entraîner l'instant d'après dans une plus grande complicité, ces impulsions émanent de telles profondeurs qu'elles continuent de nous surprendre film après film. Selon James Baldwin, le public attend d'un comédien de théâtre qu'il *joue* et d'un acteur de cinéma qu'il *soit*. « Être ou ne pas être », la grande question d'Hamlet, n'a pas besoin d'être prononcée à haute voix par Brando. Il l'incarne à chaque instant par sa fascinante présence.

STILL FROM 'LARRY KING LIVE' (1999)
"Kiss me, Larry." / „Küss mich, Larry." / « Embrasse-moi, Larry. »

2

VISUAL FILMOGRAPHY

FILMOGRAFIE IN BILDERN
FILMOGRAPHIE EN IMAGES

THE METHOD

DIE „METHODE"

LA MÉTHODE

FROM THE PLAY 'TRUCKLINE CAFÉ' (1946)
Before 'Streetcar' made him a name, Brando sparked
a sensation in this little play. / Bevor er sich mit
Endstation Sehnsucht einen Namen machte, löste
Brando schon in diesem kleinen Stück eine Sensation
aus. / Avant de se faire un nom avec *Un tramway
nommé désir*, Brando suscite l'émoi dans cette petite
pièce.

PAGE 22
MARLON BRANDO (1950)
An offbeat American archetype of the period –
the surly rebel. / Ein ausgefallener amerikanischer
Archetyp in seiner Zeit: der schroffe Rebell. /
Un archétype de l'Amérique des années 1950 :
le rebelle à la moue boudeuse.

*"The only thing an actor owes his public is not to
bore them."*
Marlon Brando

*„Das Einzige, was ein Schauspieler seinem
Publikum schuldet, ist, es nicht zu langweilen."*
Marlon Brando

FROM THE PLAY 'TRUCKLINE CAFÉ' (1946)
Critic Pauline Kael mistakenly believed young Brando
was having a seizure onstage, his acting was so vivid. /
Die Kritikerin Pauline Kael glaubte irrtümlich, der junge
Brando habe einen Anfall auf der Bühne – so intensiv
war sein Spiel. / Devant son jeu plus vrai que nature, la
critique Pauline Kael croit que le jeune acteur est
réellement victime d'une attaque.

PAGES 26/27
STILL FROM 'THE MEN' (1950)
Wounded in battle, paralyzed from the waist down –
Brando relished the challenge of playing this
character. / Kriegsversehrt und von der Hüfte abwärts
gelähmt – Brando genoss die Herausforderung, diese
Figur zu spielen. / Un défi pour Brando : le rôle d'un
homme paralysé des deux jambes après avoir été
blessé au combat.

*« La seule chose qu'un acteur doit à son public est
de ne pas l'ennuyer. »*
Marlon Brando

STILL FROM 'THE MEN' (1950)
Few film actors before Brando communicated a man's
inner life so sensitively. / Vor Brando hatten nur wenige
Schauspieler das Innenleben eines Mannes so sensibel
dargestellt. / Peu d'acteurs avant lui ont su si bien
exprimer la vie intérieure de leurs personnages.

"The more sensitive you are, the more likely you
are to be brutalized, develop scabs and never
evolve. Never allow yourself to feel anything
because you always feel too much."
Marlon Brando

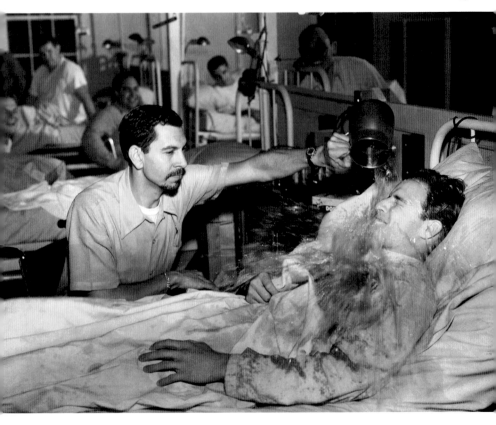

STILL FROM 'THE MEN' (1950)
Jack Webb, as a fellow disabled vet, knows just the cure for self-pity. / Jack Webb, der ebenfalls einen kriegsversehrten Veteranen spielt, weiß, was gegen Selbstmitleid hilft. / Jack Webb, autre soldat rendu infirme, l'empêche de s'apitoyer sur son sort.

„Je sensibler man ist, desto wahrscheinlicher ist es, dass man brutal behandelt wird, Schorfwunden bekommt und auf der Stelle tritt. Lass nie zu, dass du etwas fühlst, denn du fühlst immer zu viel."
Marlon Brando

« Plus on est sensible, plus on a de chances d'être brutalisé, d'avoir des cicatrices et de ne jamais évoluer. Ne vous autorisez jamais à ressentir quoi que ce soit, car ce serait toujours trop. »
Marlon Brando

STILL FROM 'THE MEN' (1950)
"Bud" (Brando) pleases his girl (Teresa Wright) by
strengthening his upper body. / „Bud" (Brando) macht
seiner Freundin (Teresa Wright) eine Freude, indem er
seinen Oberkörper stählt. / Pour plaire à sa bien-aimée
(Teresa Wright), « Bud » (Brando) se muscle le haut du
corps.

STILL FROM 'THE MEN' (1950)
Even cut in half, "Bud" is still a fighter, and suffers no
fools. / Selbst gelähmt ist „Bud" noch ein Kämpfer, der
keine Trottel duldet. / Même paralysé, « Bud » sait
encore se défendre, surtout contre les imbéciles qu'il
ne supporte pas.

"Stanley Kowalski was always right, and never afraid. He never wondered, he never doubted. His ego was very secure. And he had the kind of brutal aggressiveness that I hate. I'm afraid of it. I detest the character."
Marlon Brando

„Stanley Kowalski hatte immer Recht und nie Angst. Er wurde nie von Fragen oder Zweifeln geplagt. Sein Ego war sehr sicher. Und er besaß die Art brutaler Aggressivität, die ich hasse. Ich fürchte mich davor. Ich verabscheue diese Figur."
Marlon Brando

« Stanley Kowalski avait toujours raison et n'avait jamais peur. Il ne se posait jamais de questions, il ne doutait de rien. Il était très sûr de lui. Et il possédait une sorte d'agressivité brutale dont j'ai horreur. Ça me fait peur. Je déteste ce personnage. »
Marlon Brando

COSTUME TEST FOR 'A STREETCAR NAMED DESIRE' (1951)
Watch out, world. Here is the film role that introduced Marlon Brando as a force of nature. / Aufgepasst – hier ist die Filmrolle, mit der sich Marlon Brando als Naturereignis etablierte. / Le rôle qui fera de Marlon Brando un monstre sacré.

*"Many of the men I've like best have had strong
'feminine' characteristics: Tennessee Williams,
Clifford Odets... Budd Schulberg, Harold Clurman,
Marlon Brando... The actresses I've worked with
are, with the exception of one man, Brando, better
artists, and that is because their feelings are
concerned with their intimate life. Men have to be
constantly proving something that is often not
worth proving – their muscles, their fearlessness,
the strength of their erections..."*
Elia Kazan, 'A Life'

*„Viele der Männer, die ich am meisten mag, hatten
stark ‚feminine' Züge: Tennessee Williams, Clifford
Odets ... Budd Schulberg, Harold Clurman, Marlon
Brando ... Die Schauspielerinnen, mit denen ich
gearbeitet habe, sind – wenn man von einem Mann,
nämlich Brando, absieht – bessere Künstler, und
zwar, weil sich ihre Gefühle um ihr Innenleben
drehen. Männer müssen ständig etwas unter
Beweis stellen, das es oft nicht wert ist, bewiesen
zu werden: ihre Muskeln, ihre Furchtlosigkeit,
die Stärke ihrer Erektionen ..."*
Elia Kazan, *A Life*

**PORTRAIT FOR 'A STREETCAR NAMED
DESIRE' (1951)**
With Vivien Leigh, whose Blanche DuBois fully matched
his Stanley Kowalski, thunderbolt for thunderbolt. /
Mit Vivien Leigh, deren Blanche DuBois seinem
Stanley Kowalski in jeder Hinsicht ebenbürtig war:
Donnerschlag für Donnerschlag. / Avec Blanche DuBois
(Vivien Leigh), personnage aussi volcanique que celui de
Stanley Kowalski.

*« Les hommes que j'ai le plus appréciés
possédaient souvent de fortes caractéristiques
'féminines' : Tennessee Williams, Clifford Odets, [...]
Budd Schulberg, Harold Clurman, Marlon Brando.
À l'exception d'un homme – Brando –, les actrices
avec lesquelles j'ai travaillé sont de meilleures
artistes, car leurs sentiments portent sur leur vie
intime. Les hommes s'efforcent constamment de
prouver quelque chose qui est souvent sans
importance : leurs muscles, leur vaillance,
la puissance de leur érection... »*
Elia Kazan, *A Life*

STILL FROM 'A STREETCAR NAMED DESIRE'
(1951)
Stanley and his sister-in-law Blanche are locked in a fatal
power struggle. / Stanley und seine Schwägerin Blanche
liefern sich einen tödlichen Machtkampf. / Stanley et sa
belle-sœur Blanche, engagés dans une tragique lutte de
pouvoir.

*"I don't know what people expect when they meet
me. They seem to be afraid that I'm going to piss in
the potted palm and slap them on the ass."*
Marlon Brando

*„Ich weiß nicht, was die Leute erwarten, wenn sie
mich kennenlernen. Sie scheinen Angst zu haben,
dass ich ihnen in die Topfpflanzen pisse oder ihnen
auf den Arsch klopfe."*
Marlon Brando

**STILL FROM 'A STREETCAR NAMED DESIRE'
(1951)**
Stella (Kim Stanley) may be Blanche's sister, but is
helpless against Stanley's brute charisma. / Stella
(Kim Stanley) mag zwar Blanches Schwester sein, doch
Stanleys brutalem Charisma ist sie hilflos ausgeliefert. /
Stella (Kim Stanley), la sœur de Blanche, ne fait pas le
poids face au charisme brutal de Stanley.

*« Je ne sais pas à quoi les gens s'attendent quand
ils me rencontrent. On dirait qu'ils ont peur que je
pisse dans leur pot de fleurs et que je leur tape sur
les fesses. »*
Marlon Brando

"Even today I meet people who think of me automatically as a tough, insensitive, coarse guy named Stanley Kowalski. They can't help it, but, it is troubling."
Marlon Brando

„Selbst heute treffe ich noch Leute, die mich automatisch für einen grobschlächtigen, gefühllosen, raubeinigen Kerl namens Stanley Kowalski halten. Sie können nichts dafür, aber es macht mir Sorgen."
Marlon Brando

« Aujourd'hui encore, je rencontre des gens qui me voient automatiquement comme un type dur, insensible et grossier nommé Stanley Kowalski. C'est plus fort qu'eux, mais cela me perturbe. »
Marlon Brando

STILL FROM 'A STREETCAR NAMED DESIRE' (1951)
Seized by Kim Stanley. Playwright Tennessee Williams understood well the tragic fact that people nearly always put their most desperate needs first. / Von Kim Stanley gepackt. Dramaturg Tennessee Williams verstand die tragische Tatsache sehr gut, dass die Menschen ihren aussichtslosesten Bedürfnissen fast immer Vorrang einräumen. / Dans les bras de Kim Stanley. Pour le dramaturge Tennessee Williams, nos besoins les plus désespérés passent toujours en premier.

PAGE 40
ON THE SET OF 'A STREETCAR NAMED DESIRE' (1951)
The torn T-shirt became Brando's symbol, a calling card as sexually explicit as Marilyn Monroe's décolleté, or Elvis Presley's pelvis. / Das zerrissene T-Shirt wurde zum Symbol für Brando , zu einer sexuell eindeutigen Visitenkarte, ähnlich dem Dekolleté von Marilyn Monroe oder dem Becken von Elvis Presley. / Le T-shirt déchiré qui devient la signature de Brando, symbole aussi explicite que le décolleté de Marilyn ou les déhanchements d'Elvis.

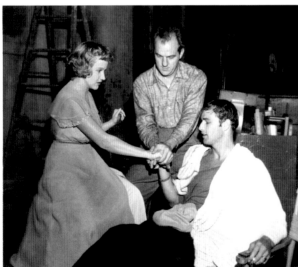

ON THE SET OF 'A STREETCAR NAMED DESIRE' (1951)
Holding hands with Kim Stanley (left) and Karl Malden (center). / Händehaltend mit Kim Stanley (links) und Karl Malden (Mitte). / Main dans la main avec Kim Stanley (à gauche) et Karl Malden (au centre).

ON THE SET OF 'A STREETCAR NAMED DESIRE' (1951)
A quick meal with Vivien Leigh (left) and Kim Stanley (right). / Eine schnelle Zwischenmahlzeit mit Vivien Leigh (links) und Kim Stanley (rechts). / Repas sur le pouce avec Vivien Leigh (à gauche) et Kim Stanley (à droite).

It Isn't That I Don't Like Glamour

No matter what they say about him, Marlon Brando refuses to conform to the accepted

By Gladys Hall

IT isn't, either—isn't that Marlon doesn't like glamour girls. I mean, as has been so often, and erroneously, reported. It's weirder than that. It's that Marlon doesn't know any glamour girls so how can he tell whether he likes them or not? Or, if he does know any glamour girls he doesn't know that he knows them because Marlon isn't quite clear, in his mind, as to what, exactly, a glamour girl is. Or have you lost me?

If you have, it's perfectly understandable. I feel rather lost myself as I sit here attempting to write a piece about a young man who requires the pen of a Proust, the probe of a psychoanalyst, or both, to do him justice.

I understand—it's my business to understand—what makes the Thesps tick and, in most cases, I do understand. Peter Lawford, for an instance, Farley Granger for another . . . young actors who, while doing right smart at their jobs, also enjoy the perquisites of their fame-names and popularity. Enjoy living well, dressing well, dining and dancing at the best bistros, dating the glamour girls, pick of the crop. Peter knows the glamour girls, he sure does, and knows that he knows them, their addresses, their telephone numbers, their middle names. Farley, although slightly less social than Peter in his tastes and habits, also dresses well, lives attractively in his

own home, appears to *be* at home under the cardboard moon that shines o'er Hollywood, and dates his normal quota. (*Shelley Winters, one of Farley's steadier dates is a full quota, one might say, in her own magnetized person!*)

Such young men as these, I know about—but Montgomery Clift, who

boasts that he owns but one suit of clothes, who eats raw meat rather than bother to cook, or buy a meal, and Marlon Brando, who sees the seasons through in a beat-up raincoat, eats but "one and one-half meals a day," and won't eat the one and a half in any place where he has to wear a tie. Marlon who doesn't know

Kim Hunter and Marlon Brando in the Broadway hit, "Streetcar Named Desire."

Girls

A romantic interlude in "The Men." "I don't run true to type," concedes Marlon.

Hollywood social pattern

a glamour girl from Grandma Moses—these boys shouldn't happen to a workaday reporter brought up, so to speak, on Van Johnson's sport coats, luncheons at the Stork with Gregory Peck, fellers who bare their fangs at mention of Lana Turner.

Why, even when we sought to enlighten Marlon concerning the glamour girls and who they are by means of naming names—Lana Turner, we said, Ava Gardner, Rita Hayworth, young Liz Taylor, Hedy Lamarr—we drew a blank.

It literally doesn't seem possible that there breathes a man, a young man, too, who registers nothing-minus when you mention Ava, Lana, Liz and the luscious like, but there does and the name's Brando.

"I don't see many movies so I'm really not familiar," Marlon explained himself, and just in time, too, "with a lot of film actors and actresses. Of the few actors with whom I am familiar, and they are very few, I admire Charlie Chaplin the

[Continued on page 67]

★ Newest Hits in Blouses from Hollywood ★

PAGES 42/43
ARTICLE FROM 'MODERN SCREEN' (1950)
Audiences viewed him as a charming enigma. /
Das Publikum betrachtete ihn als charmant und
rätselhaft. / Le public le considère comme une
charmante énigme.

"[Academy Awards are] a part of the sickness in
America, that you have to think in terms of who
wins, who loses, who's good, who's bad, who's best,
who's worst... I don't like to think that way.
Everybody has their own value in different ways,
and I don't like to think who's the best at this.
I mean, what's the point of it?"
Marlon Brando

„[Academy Awards sind] ein Teil der Krankheit in
Amerika, dass man in Kategorien von Gewinnern
und Verlierern denkt, wer gut ist und wer schlecht,
wer der Beste und wer der Schlechteste ... Ich mag
nicht so denken. Jeder besitzt auf unterschiedliche
Weise eigene Werte, und ich mag nicht daran
denken, wer dabei der Beste ist. Ich meine - was
soll's?"
Marlon Brando

« [Les Oscars sont] un élément du mal qui ronge
l'Amérique, le fait qu'on soit obligé de penser en
termes de vainqueur et de perdant, de bon et de
méchant, de pire et de meilleur... Je n'aime pas
penser en ces termes. Chacun a de la valeur à sa
manière et je n'aime pas me demander qui est le
meilleur. À quoi ça sert ? »
Marlon Brando

PORTRAIT FOR 'VIVA ZAPATA!' (1952)
At one point in the production, Brando accidentally
swallowed his brown contact lenses. / Während der
Dreharbeiten verschluckte Brando einmal versehentlich
seine braunen Haftschalen. / Lors du tournage, Brando
avale accidentellement ses lentilles de contact marron.

STILL FROM 'VIVA ZAPATA!' (1952)
In latter years, critics have questioned whether it was
appropriate to cast a norteamericano in this role,
but Brando has the great Zapata's warmth and
spontaneity. / In jüngerer Zeit haben Kritiker die Frage
aufgeworfen, ob es angemessen war, einen
„norteamericano" diese Rolle spielen zu lassen, doch
Brando besaß durchaus die Wärme und Spontaneität
des großen Zapata. / Par la suite, les critiques
remettront en cause le choix d'un « norteamericano »
pour ce rôle, mais Brando possède la chaleur et
la spontanéité du grand Zapata.

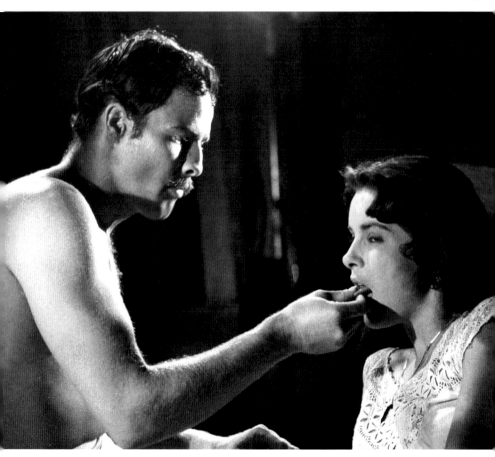

STILL FROM 'VIVA ZAPATA!' (1952)
Zapata feeding his bride (Jean Peters) on their wedding
night: a moment of tenderest communion, literally and
figuratively. / Zapata füttert seine Braut (Jean Peters)
in der Hochzeitsnacht: ein Augenblick zärtlichster
Kommunion, sowohl wörtlich wie auch im übertragenen
Sinne. / Instant de communion : Zapata donnant la
becquée à sa femme (Jean Peters) pendant leur nuit de
noces.

"An actor is at most a poet and at least an entertainer."
Marlon Brando

„Ein Schauspieler ist bestenfalls ein Poet und mindestens ein Unterhalter."
Marlon Brando

« Un acteur se doit au mieux d'être un poète et au pire de vous distraire. »
Marlon Brando

STILL FROM 'JULIUS CAESAR' (1953)
"Friends, Romans, Countrymen!" If anyone doubted Brando's greatness of range, his brief but volatile appearance here as Mark Antony proved him to be the actor of his generation, and beyond. / „Freunde, Römer, Landsleute!" Sollte irgendjemand jemals an Brandos schauspielerischer Bandbreite gezweifelt haben, so bewies sein ebenso kurzer wie lebhafter Auftritt als Mark Anton hier, dass er der Schauspieler seiner Generation war – und darüber hinaus. / « Amis, Romains, compatriotes ! » Si l'on doutait de l'ampleur de son talent, sa brève apparition dans le rôle de Marc-Antoine prouve qu'il est le plus grand acteur de sa génération.

ON THE SET OF 'JULIUS CAESAR' (1953)
Matched heavyweights, left to right: John Gielgud,
Brando, James Mason, director Joseph Mankiewicz and
(as Caesar) Louis Calhern. / Schwergewichte, die
zueinander passen, von links nach rechts: John Gielgud,
Brando, James Mason, Regisseur Joseph Mankiewicz
und (als Caesar) Louis Calhern. / Un parterre de poids
lourds, de gauche à droite : John Gielgud, Marlon
Brando, James Mason, le réalisateur Joseph Mankiewicz
et Louis Calhern (en César).

ON THE SET OF 'JULIUS CAESAR' (1953)
Geared for battle as the crew readies the next
setup. / Kampfbereit – während die Techniker die
nächste Einstellung vorbereiten. / Paré pour la bataille
tandis que les techniciens s'affairent avant la prochaine
prise.

PAGES 52/53
ON THE SET OF 'JULIUS CAESAR' (1953)
Brushing up on his Shakespeare. / Schlag nach bei
Shakespeare! / Révisant Shakespeare.

STILL FROM 'THE WILD ONE' (1954)
Defying censors and just good manners by pulling at his
leading lady, Mary Murphy. / Hier setzt er sich über die
Zensur und schlichtweg gute Manieren hinweg, indem
er an der Hauptdarstellerin (Mary Murphy) zupft. / Défi-
ant la censure et les bonnes manières avec sa partenaire Mary Murphy.

PORTRAIT FOR 'THE WILD ONE' (1954)
The first motorcycle outlaws were often World War Two
veterans – note the "uniform without a country." / Die
ersten Gesetzlosen auf Motorrädern waren oft
Veteranen des Zweiten Weltkriegs – man beachte die
„staatenlose Uniform". / Les premiers blousons noirs
sont souvent d'anciens combattants arborant désormais
un « uniforme apatride ».

STILL FROM 'THE WILD ONE' (1954)
Our freewheeling rebel falls afoul of some vengeance-minded locals. / Unser freier und ungebundener Rebell gerät in Konflikt mit rachelüsternen Bürgern. / Notre insouciant rebelle se heurte à la colère des habitants prêts à en découdre.

PORTRAIT FOR 'THE WILD ONE' (1954)
Brando sincerely hoped to explore a social crisis, but the film only made outlaw bikers look sexy. / Brando hatte ernsthaft gehofft, auf eine gesellschaftliche Krise eingehen zu können, doch durch den Film wirkten Motorradbanditen einfach nur sexy. / Alors que Brando espérait une étude sociale, le film se contente de donner une image sexy des motards.

ON THE SET OF 'THE WILD ONE' (1954)
Taking a note from director Lazlo Benedek. / Er nimmt
eine Anweisung von Regisseur Lazlo Benedek
entgegen. / Attentif aux instructions de Lazlo Benedek.

PORTRAIT FOR 'THE WILD ONE' (1954)
Posed with his gang of latter-day Western Outlaws. /
Hier posiert er mit seiner Bande moderner
Westernbanditen. / Johnny et sa bande de cow-boys
des temps modernes.

"What are you rebelling against, Johnny?"
"What'ch you got?"
'The Wild One'

„Wogegen lehnst du dich auf, Johnny?"
„Was kannst du mir denn anbieten?"
Der Wilde

« Contre quoi te rebelles-tu, Johnny ? »
« Qu'est-ce tu me proposes ? »
L'Équipée sauvage

60

ON THE SET OF 'ON THE WATERFRONT' (1954)
"A pigeon for a pigeon." This drama of giving testimony
was of personal importance to director Elia Kazan
(right). / „Taube um Taube." Dieses Drama zum Thema
Zeugenaussagen hatte für Regisseur Elia Kazan (rechts)
auch persönliche Bedeutung. / « Un pigeon pour
un pigeon. » Un cas de conscience qui tient
personnellement à cœur au réalisateur Elia Kazan
(à droite).

STILL FROM 'ON THE WATERFRONT' (1954)
Enmeshed, however tenderly, with co-star Eva Marie
Saint. / In einem – wenn auch zarten – Netz gefangen
mit Eva Marie Saint, die hier die weibliche Hauptrolle
spielt. / Pris au filet en charmante compagnie de sa
partenaire Eva Marie Saint.

STILL FROM 'ON THE WATERFRONT' (1954)
Terry Malloy (Brando), the fighter who sold out, now
fiercely defends his own integrity. / Terry Malloy
(Brando), der sich als Boxer kaufen ließ, verteidigt nun
heftig seine Integrität. / Terry Malloy (Brando), l'ancien
boxeur passé dans l'autre camp, défend farouchement
son intégrité.

STILL FROM 'ON THE WATERFRONT' (1954)
With Eva Marie Saint. Both are in danger of being
silenced by mobsters. / Mit Eva Marie Saint. Beide sind
in Gefahr, von Gangstern zum Schweigen gebracht zu
werden. / Avec Eva Marie Saint, il tente d'échapper aux
truands qui veulent les faire taire.

PAGES 64/65
STILL FROM 'ON THE WATERFRONT' (1954)
Karl Malden (right) speaks for Terry's conscience in this
morality play. / Karl Malden (rechts) ist in diesem
Moraldrama Terrys Gewissensstimme. / Dans ce drame
moral, le père Barry (Karl Malden) est la voix de la
conscience de Terry.

STILL FROM 'ON THE WATERFRONT' (1954)
Lee J. Cobb (left) is restrained against killing the
truthful Terry (Brando, right). / Johnny (Lee J. Cobb,
links) wird daran gehindert, den aufrichtigen Terry
(Brando, rechts) zu töten. / Johnny (Lee J. Cobb, à
gauche) veut la faire la peau au renégat, mais il en est
empêché.

"'This ain't your night.' My night! I coulda taken
Wilson apart! So what happens? He gets the title
shot outdoors on a ball park, and what do I get?
A one-way ticket to Palookaville. ... I could've had
class! I could've been a contender. I could've been
somebody! Instead of a bum, which is what I am.
Let's face it."
Terry Malloy, 'On the Waterfront'

„,Das ist nicht deine Nacht.' Meine Nacht!
Ich hätte Wilson auseinandernehmen können!
Aber was passiert? Er bekommt die Chance auf
den Titel in einem Stadion unter freiem Himmel
und ich werde in die Versenkung geschickt – ohne
Rückfahrkarte ... Ich hätte Klasse haben können!
Ich hätte um den Titel kämpfen können! Ich hätte
wer sein können! Statt des Niemands, der ich jetzt
bin. Seien wir doch ehrlich."
Terry Malloy, _Die Faust im Nacken_

STILL FROM 'ON THE WATERFRONT' (1954)
Neither Rod Steiger (left) nor Brando felt it was truthful for one brother to draw a gun on another – so they brilliantly incorporated this disbelief into the scene. / Weder Rod Steiger (links) noch Brando hielten es für realistisch, dass ein Bruder den anderen mit der Waffe bedrohen würde – und sie bauten ihre Ansicht daher auf geniale Weise in diese Szene ein. / Peu convaincus de la véracité de la scène où Charley (Rod Steiger, à gauche) pointe son arme sur son frère, les deux acteurs intègrent intelligemment leur incrédulité dans les dialogues.

« "C'est pas ton jour." Pas mon jour ! J'aurais pu lui faire la peau, à Wilson ! Et au lieu de ça ? Il décroche un match pour le titre dans un stade, et moi, qu'est-ce que j'ai ? Un aller simple pour Trifouilly-les-Oies. [...] J'aurais pu avoir de la classe ! J'aurais pu être un prétendant au titre. J'aurais pu être quelqu'un ! Et pas un clodo, car c'est ce que je suis maintenant, il faut voir les choses en face. »
Terry Malloy, *Sur les quais*

ON THE SET OF 'ON THE WATERFRONT' (1954)
Brando was angry at Kazan (left) over the director's
'friendly testimony' to the US congress regarding
Communist activities. The director had to plead with
him to accept the role. / Brando war wütend auf Kazan
(links), weil der Regisseur vor dem Kongressausschuss
zur Untersuchung unamerikanischer Aktivitäten
zugunsten der Kommunistenjäger ausgesagt hatte.
Der Regisseur musste daher betteln, dass er die Rolle
annahm. / Elia Kazan (à gauche) devra insister pour faire
accepter ce rôle à Brando, qui lui en veut d'avoir
témoigné contre les communistes devant le Congrès.

STILL FROM 'ON THE WATERFRONT' (1954)
Lee J. Cobb turns Terry's first day back at work into a
Christ-like ordeal. / Johnny Friendly (Lee J. Cobb)
verwandelt Terrys ersten neuen Arbeitstag in eine
christusähnliche Leidensgeschichte. / Johnny (Lee J.
Cobb) lui fait payer cher d'avoir brisé la loi du silence.

STILL FROM 'DÉSIRÉE' (1954)
Sexily confronting Jean Simmons: "Have you ever heard of a thing called Destiny, Désirée?" / Sexuelle An-näherung gegenüber Jean Simmons: „Habt Ihr schon einmal von einer Sache namens Schicksal gehört, Désirée?" / À la conquête de Jean Simmons : « Avez-vous déjà entendu parler du destin, Désirée ? »

PORTRAIT FOR 'DÉSIRÉE' (1954)
Where is Stanley Kubrick when we need him? Brando is an ideal Napoleon, but needed an ideal director. / Wo ist Stanley Kubrick, wenn man ihn braucht? Brando ist ein idealer Napoleon, aber er hätte einen ebenso idealen Regisseur gebrauchen können. / Il aurait fallu un cinéaste de l'envergure de Stanley Kubrick pour filmer Brando en Napoléon plus vrai que nature.

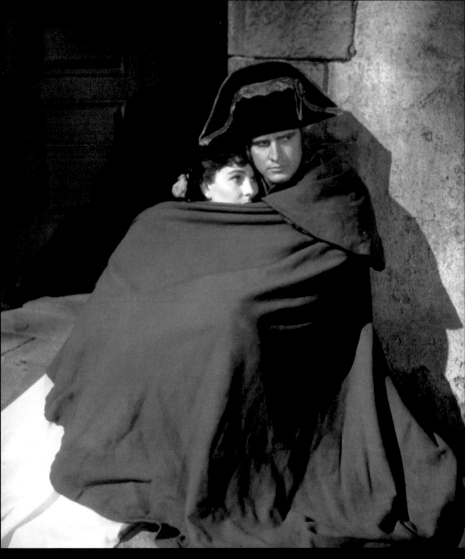

PORTRAIT FOR 'DÉSIRÉE' (1954)
Brando had defied studio boss Darryl Zanuck.
Forcing him to accept this role was Zanuck's revenge. /
Brando hatte Studioboss Darryl Zanuck die Stirn
geboten. Dieser rächte sich, indem er Brando zwang,
diese Rolle anzunehmen. / Pour le punir de l'avoir défié,
Darryl Zanuck, patron de la Fox, contraint Brando à
accepter ce rôle.

STILL FROM 'DÉSIRÉE' (1954)
The life of Napoleon, as remembered by a beauty (Jean
Simmons) whom he dumped on the path to greatness. /
Das Leben Napoleons in der Erinnerung einer
Schönheit (Jean Simmons), die er auf dem Weg zum
Ruhm fallenließ wie eine heiße Kartoffel. / La vie de
Napoléon racontée par la belle (Jean Simmons) qu'il a
abandonnée sur le chemin de la gloire.

IMPONDERABLES

UNWÄGBARKEITEN

LES IMPONDÉRABLES

PAGE 74
PORTRAIT FOR 'GUYS AND DOLLS' (1955)

STILL FROM 'GUYS AND DOLLS' (1955)
Brando and Jean Simmons worked together
wonderfully in this classic, from the stories of Damon
Runyon. / Brando und Jean Simmons arbeiteten in
diesem Klassiker nach den Geschichten von Damon
Runyon wunderbar zusammen. / Brando et Jean Simmons s'accordent à merveille dans ce classique tiré
d'une histoire de Damon Runyon.

STILL FROM 'GUYS AND DOLLS' (1955)
Garbo merely talked, but Brando? "He sings!"
A delightful venture into musical comedy, again
opposite Jean Simmons. / Garbo sprach nur, aber
Brando? „Er singt!" Ein unterhaltsamer Ausflug in die
musikalische Komödie, wieder an der Seite von Jean
Simmons. / Garbo parlait, Brando chante ! Aux côtés de
Jean Simmons dans une délicieuse comédie musicale.

STILL FROM 'GUYS AND DOLLS' (1955)
Sky Masterson (Brando) is a gangster in love with a very
proper lady (Simmons) of the Salvation Army. / Sky
Masterson (Brando) ist ein Gangster, der sich in eine
sehr anständige Dame (Simmons) von der Heilsarmee
verliebt hat. / Sky Masterson (Brando), gangster
épris d'une jeune femme de l'Armée du Salut (Jean
Simmons).

*"An actor's a guy who, if you ain't talking about
him, ain't listening."*
Marlon Brando

*„Ein Schauspieler ist ein Typ, der nur zuhört, wenn
man über ihn redet."*
Marlon Brando

*« Un acteur, c'est quelqu'un qui n'écoute que quand
on parle de lui. »*
Marlon Brando

STILL FROM 'GUYS AND DOLLS' (1955)
"Luck, Be a Lady Tonight ..." Brando performs the song
that became the lovely signature of this musical. /
„Luck, Be a Lady Tonight ...": Brando singt das Lied, das
zur Erkennungsmelodie dieses Musicals wurde. /
Brando interprète *Luck, Be a Lady Tonight ...*, la chanson
phare du film.

ON THE SET OF 'GUYS AND DOLLS' (1955)
Dealing with a special assistant: 'Brando's old chewing
gum in here,' reads the sign. / Ein ganz besonderer
Assistent: „Brandos alter Kaugummi hier rein" steht auf
dem Schild. / Aux côtés d'un assistant tribalant un
crachoir destiné spécialement au « vieux chewing-gum
de Brando ».

STILL FROM 'GUYS AND DOLLS' (1955)
Underworld Boss weds Heavenly Beauty – Broadway
style: Jean Simmons and Marlon Brando. / Boss der
Unterwelt heiratet himmlische Schönheit – im
Broadway-Stil: Jean Simmons und Marlon Brando. /
Les noces du caïd (Marlon Brando) et de la colombe
(Jean Simmons) à la mode de Broadway.

82

**STILL FROM 'THE TEAHOUSE OF THE
AUGUST MOON' (1956)**
Brando (left) as the clever Okinawan interpreter Sakini,
who persuades American officers (including Glenn
Ford, center) to 'go native.' / Brando (links) als Sakini,
der schlaue Dolmetscher aus Okinawa, überredet die
amerikanischen Offiziere (darunter Glenn Ford, Mitte),
sich den Einheimischen anzupassen. / Brando
(à gauche) dans le rôle de l'interprète Sakini, qui
persuade des officiers américains (dont Glenn Ford,
au centre) d'adopter les coutumes locales.

STILL FROM 'THE TEAHOUSE OF THE AUGUST MOON' (1956)
Some moviegoers complained, "Where was Marlon Brando?" They were shocked to be told he had been onscreen for most of the movie. / Einige Kinobesucher beschwerten sich nach dem Film, weil sie Brando nicht gefunden hatten, und waren überrascht, als sie hörten, dass er den größten Teil des Films auf der Leinwand gewesen war. / Marlon Brando est tellement méconnaissable que certains spectateurs ressortent de la salle sans l'avoir reconnu.

STILL FROM 'SAYONARA' (1957)
A contemplative moment, as a soldier overwhelmed by the land his army has occupied. / Ein Augenblick der Nachdenklichkeit, als ein Soldat von dem Land überwältigt wird, das seine Armee besetzt hat. / Instant de contemplation d'un soldat bouleversé par le pays que son armée vient d'occuper.

STILL FROM 'SAYONARA' (1957)
As a US Air Force major in love with a Japanese woman (Miko Taka). / Ein Major der US-Luftwaffe, der sich in eine Japanerin (Miko Taka) verliebt hat. / En pilote américain tombé amoureux d'une Japonaise (Miko Taka).

STILL FROM 'SAYONARA' (1957)
Miko Taka (left), embodying the enormous
transformation of Japan after World War Two. / Miko
Taka (links) verkörpert die enorme Wandlung Japans
nach dem Zweiten Weltkrieg. / Miko Taka (à gauche)
incarne la prodigieuse transformation du Japon
d'après-guerre.

POSTER FOR 'SAYONARA' (1957)
Socially conscious, passionate about Civil Rights,
Brando gladly starred in this interracial love story. /
Mit seinem sozialen Gewissen und seiner Passion für
Bürgerrechte spielte Brando gern die Hauptrolle in
dieser gemischtrassigen Liebesgeschichte. / Épris de
justice sociale et fervent défenseur des droits civiques,
Brando accepte volontiers cette histoire d'amour
interraciale.

STILL FROM 'THE YOUNG LIONS' (1958)
Comforting a wounded comrade (Maximilian Schell,
under bandages) before coldly putting him out of his
misery. / Zuerst tröstet er einen verwundeten
Kameraden (Maximilian Schell, mit Verband), bevor
er ihn eiskalt aus seinem Elend erlöst. / Il réconforte un
camarade blessé (Maximilian Schell) avant d'abréger
froidement ses souffrances.

PORTRAIT FOR 'THE YOUNG LIONS' (1958)
As Lt. Christian Diestl, novelist Irwin Shaw's complex
Nazi. / Als Leutnant Christian Diestl, der komplexe
Nationalsozialist aus der Feder des Romanautors Irwin
Shaw. / Dans le rôle complexe de l'officier nazi Christian
Diestl, d'après un roman d'Irwin Shaw.

STILL FROM 'THE YOUNG LIONS' (1958)
Fleeing a lost battle, with Maximilian Schell (right):
"I wish I was in the mountains, skiing," Diestl says
quietly. / Auf der Flucht nach einer verlorenen Schlacht,
mit Maximilian Schell (rechts): „Ich wünschte, ich wäre
in den Bergen, beim Skifahren", murmelt Diestl. /
Fuyant une bataille perdue avec Maximilian Schell
(à droite) : « J'aimerais être à la montagne en train de
faire du ski. »

ON THE SET OF 'THE YOUNG LIONS' (1958)
Taking direction from Edward Dmytryk, before the
climactic showdown. / Vor dem großen Showdown
erhält er noch einmal Regieanweisungen von Edward
Dmytryk. / Derniers conseils du réalisateur Edward
Dmytryk avant la scène finale.

ON THE SET OF 'THE FUGITIVE KIND' (1960)
Paired with Anna Magnani, whom many critics honored
as his female equivalent in talent, and passion. / Zusammen mit Anna Magnani, nach Meinung vieler Kritiker
ihm ebenbürtig in Begabung und Leidenschaft. / Avec
Anna Magnani, que de nombreux critiques considèrent
comme son égale en termes de talent et de fougue.

STILL FROM 'THE FUGITIVE KIND' (1960)
As Valentine "Snakeskin" Xavier, a role created
specifically for him by Tennessee Williams. / Die Rolle
des Valentine „Snakeskin" Xavier wurde ihm von
Tennessee Williams eigens auf den Leib geschrieben. /
« L'homme à la peau de serpent », un rôle créé
spécialement pour lui par Tennessee Williams.

STILL FROM 'THE FUGITIVE KIND' (1960)

The hero's snakeskin jacket is a memorably physical, sexy expression of his inner life – later fondly spoofed by director David Lynch in his 1989 film, 'Wild at Heart.' / Die Jacke aus Schlangenleder, die der Held trägt, ist ein markanter erotischer Ausdruck seines Innenlebens – von Regisseur David Lynch in seinem Film *Wild at Heart* (1989) liebevoll parodiert. / La célèbre veste en peau de serpent, expression de la personnalité du héros, que David Lynch parodiera affectueusement dans *Sailor et Lula* (1989).

"Regret is useless in life. It's in the past. All we have is now."
Marlon Brando

„Bedauern bringt im Leben nichts. Es gehört zur Vergangenheit. Alles, was wir haben, ist das Jetzt."
Marlon Brando

STILL FROM 'THE FUGITIVE KIND' (1960)
With Anna Magnani, as a pair of outsiders in a hostile
world, sharing a rare moment of peace. / Mit Anna
Magnani als Außenseiterpärchen inmitten einer feind-
seligen Welt in einem seltenen Augenblick des
Friedens. / Avec Anna Magnani, deux marginaux parta-
geant un rare instant de paix dans un monde hostile.

« Dans la vie, rien ne sert de regretter. Le passé,
c'est le passé. Nous n'avons que le présent. »
Marlon Brando

"I put on an act sometimes, and people think I'm insensitive. Really, it's like a kind of armor because I'm too sensitive. If there are two hundred people in a room and one of them doesn't like me, I've got to get out."
Marlon Brando

STILL FROM 'THE FUGITIVE KIND' (1960)
Critics expressed disappointment (at first) over a supposed lack of chemistry between Brando and Magnani, but the film remains fascinating. / Die Kritiker äußerten sich (zunächst) enttäuscht über den angeblichen Mangel an „Chemie" zwischen Brando und Magnani, doch der Film übt noch immer Faszination aus. / Bien que les critiques aient déploré que le courant ne passe pas entre Brando et Magnani, ce film demeure fascinant.

„Manchmal verstelle ich mich, und die Leute halten mich für gefühllos. In Wirklichkeit ist es eine Art Schutzschild, weil ich zu sensibel bin. Wenn zweihundert Menschen in einem Raum sind und mich einer von ihnen nicht mag, dann muss ich rausgehen."
Marlon Brando

« Parfois je me donne des airs et les gens me croient insensible. En réalité, c'est comme une armure, car je suis trop sensible. Si je suis dans une pièce avec deux cents personnes et qu'il y en a une qui ne m'aime pas, je suis obligé de sortir. »
Marlon Brando

"I [tried directing] once. It was an ass-breaker. You work yourself to death. You're the first one up in the morning... I mean, we shot [One-Eyed Jacks] on the run, you know. You make up the dialog the scene before, improvising, and your brain is going crazy."
Marlon Brando

„*Ich habe einmal versucht, Regie zu führen. Den Arsch hab ich mir dabei aufgerissen. Man arbeitet sich zu Tode. Morgens ist man als Erster auf den Beinen ... ich meine, wir haben [One-Eyed Jacks (Der Besessene/Noch hänge ich nicht)] im Laufen gedreht, wissen Sie. Man denkt sich in der Szene vorher den Dialog aus, improvisiert, und man dreht völlig durch im Gehirn.*"
Marlon Brando

« *J'ai [été réalisateur] une fois. C'était vraiment casse-cul. On se tue au travail. On est le premier debout le matin... En fait, on a tourné [La Vengeance aux deux visages] au pas de course. On invente les dialogues pendant la scène précédente, on improvise et on a le cerveau qui explose.* »
Marlon Brando

PORTRAIT FOR 'ONE-EYED JACKS' (1961)
Brando's original title for this opus was 'A Burst of Vermilion.' / Brandos ursprünglicher Titel für dieses Werk war „A Burst of Vermilion" („Ein Ausbruch von Zinnober"). / *La Vengeance aux deux visages* est le seul film mis en scène par Brando.

STILL FROM 'ONE-EYED JACKS' (1961)
With Mexican star Pina Pellicer, as the stepdaughter of
the man he means to kill. / Mit dem mexikanischen Star
Pina Pellicer als Stieftochter des Mannes, den er zu
töten beabsichtigt. / Avec la star mexicaine Pina Pellicer, qui incarne la belle-fille de l'homme dont il veut se
venger.

PORTRAIT FOR 'ONE-EYED JACKS' (1961)
As Rio, a play on Billy the Kid. / Als Rio alias „Kid". eine
Anspielung auf Billy the Kid. / Rio, alias « Kid », un per-
sonnage inspiré de Billy the Kid.

ON THE SET OF 'ONE-EYED JACKS' (1961)
Although wildly over budget and miserable amid the burdens of power, Brando proved a highly capable, imaginative director. A great pity he didn't direct more. / Obwohl er das Budget maßlos überzog und sich unter der Last der Verantwortung elend fühlte, erwies sich Brando als sehr fähiger und einfallsreicher Regisseur. Schade, dass er nicht öfter Regie führte. / Malgré un dépassement de budget astronomique et des responsabilités qui lui pèsent, Brando s'avère un réalisateur talentueux et créatif qu'on aurait aimé voir plus souvent dans ce rôle.

STILL FROM 'ONE-EYED JACKS' (1961)
Making a jailbreak with Slim Pickens on all fours and at gunpoint. / Beim Gefängnisausbruch mit Slim Pickens (auf allen vieren). / Évasion de la prison avec Slim Pickens à quatre pattes et à bout portant.

STILL FROM 'ONE-EYED JACKS' (1961)
A martyr in waiting, relaxing between beatings.
Laurence Olivier gave Brando this advice, about
directing oneself: "Use a stand-in for rehearsals who
knows how to act." / Ein Märtyrer in Wartestellung, der
sich zwischen den Prügeln entspannt. Laurence Olivier
gab Brando diesen Rat zur Doppelrolle von Regisseur
und Darsteller: „Hol dir für die Proben ein Double, das
schauspielern kann." / Un martyr prêt à se faire rouer
de coups. Pour se mettre lui-même en scène, Laurence
Olivier conseille à Brando de « répéter avec une dou-
blure qui sait jouer ».

STILL FROM 'ONE-EYED JACKS' (1961)
"Kid," being whipped by "Dad" (Karl Malden, deep center), the "Pat Garrett" figure in this iconic panorama of Western Legend. / „Kid" wird von „Dad" (Karl Malden, hinten in der Mitte) ausgepeitscht, der „Pat Garrett"-Figur in diesem symbolischen Panorama von Westernlegenden. / « Kid » se fait fouetter par « Dad » (Karl Malden, derrière lui), personnage évoquant Pat Garrett dans ce film inspiré de la légende de l'Ouest.

"If the vacuum formed by Dr. [Martin Luther] King's
death isn't filled with concern and understanding
and a measure of love, then I think we all are really
going to be lost here in this country."
Marlon Brando

„Wenn das Vakuum, das der Tod von Dr. [Martin
Luther] King hinterlassen hat, nicht mit Besorgnis
und Verständnis und einem gewissen Maß an Liebe
gefüllt wird, dann, glaube ich, werden wir hier in
diesem Land alle verloren sein."
Marlon Brando

« Si le vide laissé par la mort du Dr [Martin Luther]
King n'est pas comblé par de la compassion, de la
compréhension et une dose d'amour, je crois que
nous serons tous perdus dans ce pays. »
Marlon Brando

**PORTRAIT FOR 'MUTINY ON THE BOUNTY'
(1962)**
The role of Fletcher Christian, with his classical ele-
gance and passionate will to rebel, seemed made for
Marlon Brando. / Mit seiner klassischen Eleganz und
seiner Leidenschaft für Rebellion schien die Rolle des
Fletcher Christian Marlon Brando auf den Leib
geschrieben. / Avec son élégance classique et sa
passion de la rébellion, le rôle de Fletcher Christian est
taillé sur mesure pour Brando.

STILL FROM 'MUTINY ON THE BOUNTY' (1962)
Attempting to show mercy despite a kick of protest
from Captain Bligh (Trevor Howard, center). / Trotz
eines protestierenden Tritts von Kapitän Bligh (Trevor
Howard, Mitte) versucht er, Gnade walten zu lassen. /
Un geste de miséricorde malgré le coup de pied rageur
du capitaine Bligh (Trevor Howard, au centre).

STILL FROM 'MUTINY ON THE BOUNTY' (1962)
Defending Bligh from death at the hands of his own
crew during the mutiny. / Hier rettet er Bligh davor,
während der Meuterei von der eigenen Mannschaft
getötet zu werden. / Pendant la mutinerie, il tente
d'empêcher Bligh de se faire tuer par son propre
équipage.

ON THE SET OF 'MUTINY ON THE BOUNTY'
(1962)
Brando fell in love with Tahiti and its people, and for
decades thereafter made it his home. / Brando
verliebte sich in Tahiti und seine Bewohner und machte
es über Jahrzehnte zu seiner zweiten Heimat. / Tombé
amoureux de Tahiti et de ses habitants, Brando y vivra
ensuite pendant des décennies.

"I have always been lucky with women."
Marlon Brando

„Mit Frauen habe ich immer Glück gehabt."
Marlon Brando

« J'ai toujours eu de la chance avec les femmes. »
Marlon Brando

PORTRAIT FOR 'MUTINY ON THE BOUNTY'
(1962)
Brando with his co-star Tarita, whom he later married,
and with whom he had many children. / Brando mit
seiner Kollegin Tarita, die er später heiratete und mit
der er zahlreiche Kinder zeugte. / Brando avec sa
partenaire Tarita, avec qui il se mariera et aura
beaucoup d'enfants.

A CONTINENT AS A BATTLEGROUND AND HALF A WORLD AS A PRIZE...!

A man and an adventure to match the explosive events of our time!

Marlon Brando *in his most powerful role!* **"The Ugly American"**

in Eastman COLOR

co-starring SANDRA CHURCH · EIJI OKADA · PAT HINGLE with ARTHUR HILL

Screen Story and Screenplay by STEWART STERN · From the novel by William J. Lederer and Eugene Burdick · Produced and Directed by GEORGE ENGLUND

POSTER FOR 'THE UGLY AMERICAN' (1963)
This tale of a fictional country transparently modeled on Vietnam is still biting 40 years later, as the US policies Brando embodies so smartly here are still tragically in force. / Diese Geschichte eines erfundenen, aber offensichtlich Vietnam nachempfundenen Landes hat auch nach vier Jahrzehnten nichts von ihrem Biss verloren, zumal die US-Politik, die Brando hier so geschickt verkörpert, tragischerweise noch immer aktuell ist. / Cette fable située dans un pays imaginaire inspiré du Viêtnam reste d'actualité 40 ans après, la politique américaine incarnée ici avec brio par Brando n'ayant hélas guère changé.

STILL FROM 'THE UGLY AMERICAN' (1963)
Deong (Eiji Okada), leader of a popular movement in Southeast Asia, is assassinated in the arms of the US ambassador (Brando). / Deong (Eiji Okada), Führer einer Volksbewegung in Südostasien, wird in den Armen des US-Botschafters (Brando) ermordet. / Deong (Eiji Okada), leader d'un mouvement populaire d'Asie du Sud-Est, est assassiné dans les bras de l'ambassadeur des États-Unis (Brando).

STILL FROM 'BEDTIME STORY' (1964)
A rare jump into farce, in the role of an ambitious
conman. / Ein seltener Ausflug ins Lustspiel – in der
Rolle eines ehrgeizigen Schwindlers. / Brando
s'aventure dans l'univers de la farce en endossant le rôle
d'un escroc ambitieux.

STILL FROM 'BEDTIME STORY' (1964)
Critics underrated this classic comedy, which co-starred
David Niven (right), and has since been successfully
remade with Steve Martin and Michael Caine as 'Dirty
Rotten Scoundrels.' / Die Kritik unterschätzte diese
klassische Komödie, in der David Niven (rechts) die
andere Hauptrolle spielte und die 1988 mit Steve Martin
und Michael Caine unter dem Titel *Zwei hinreißend
verdorbene Schurken* erfolgreich neuverfilmt wurde. /
Aux côtés de David Niven (à droite) dans une comédie
sous-estimée par la critique, d'où est tiré le remake
Le Plus Escroc des deux, avec Steve Martin et Michael
Caine.

"I think of my middle age as the 'Fuck You' years.
If I met a man who had a certain kind of overt
masculinity, he became my enemy. I would find his
weakness, then exploit it. I adopted his manner
until I made a fool of him, which often took the
form of sleeping with his wife."
Marlon Brando

„Meinen mittleren Lebensabschnitt betrachte ich
als die ,Leck mich am Arsch'-Jahre. Wenn ich einen
Mann mit einer bestimmten Art offener
Männlichkeit traf, wurde er mein Feind. Ich fand
seine Schwäche heraus und nutzte sie aus. Ich hab
sein Verhalten übernommen, bis ich ihn zum Trottel
gemacht hatte, was sehr oft dadurch geschah,
dass ich mit seiner Frau schlief."
Marlon Brando

« Vers le milieu de ma vie, j'ai eu ma période
"Vas te faire foutre". Quand je rencontrais un
homme doté d'une certaine virilité affichée, j'en
faisais mon ennemi. Je trouvais son point faible et
je l'exploitais. Je me comportais comme lui jusqu'à
ce que j'arrive à le ridiculiser, ce qui consistait
souvent à coucher avec sa femme. »
Marlon Brando

ON THE SET OF 'MORITURI' (1965)
As a German in World War Two, sabotaging another
German (Yul Brynner, top) and seducing yet another
(Janet Margolin, center). / Als Deutscher im Zweiten
Weltkrieg sabotiert er einen Landsmann (Yul Brynner,
oben) und verführt eine Landsmännin (Janet Margolin,
Mitte). / Pendant la guerre, Brando incarne un Allemand
déserteur qui va saboter les plans du capitaine nazi
(Yul Brynner, en haut) et séduire une autre compatriote
(Janet Margolin, au centre).

PORTRAIT FOR 'THE CHASE' (1966)
Opposite Angie Dickinson (right), as he plays Calder, a cagey Texas sheriff. / Neben Angie Dickinson (rechts) spielt er hier Calder, einen verschlossenen Sheriff in Texas. / Aux côtés d'Angie Dickinson dans le rôle de Calder, un shérif texan désabusé.

STILL FROM 'THE CHASE' (1966)
"I'm not on patrol," he drawls off-handedly. "I'm just lookin' for an ice cream cone." / „Ich bin nicht auf Streife", nuschelt er lässig, „ich suche nur nach einer Eiswaffeltüte." / « Je ne suis pas en service, dit-il d'un ton désinvolte, je cherche juste un cornet de glace. »

STILL FROM 'THE CHASE' (1966)
Calder takes a principled stand which earns him a terrible beating. / Weil Calder seinen Prinzipien treu bleibt, muss er ordentlich Prügel einstecken. / Calder prend une position de principe qui lui vaudra un terrible passage à tabac.

STILL FROM 'THE CHASE' (1966)
Mob justice is the collective villain in this forceful allegory of American life in the mid 1960s. / Lynchjustiz ist der kollektive Übeltäter in dieser überzeugenden Allegorie über das Leben in Amerika Mitte der sechziger Jahre des vergangenen Jahrhunderts. / Une puissante allégorie de l'Amérique du milieu des années 1960 qui dénonce la violence collective.

"It is a tribute to Brando's unceasing dignity that he has striven to seem a true person on film, not gilded by attractiveness or reputation."
David Thomson

„Es zeugt von Brandos anhaltender Würde, dass er bestrebt war, im Film als wahrhaftige Person zu erscheinen, die nicht von Attraktivität oder Ansehen geschönt wird."
David Thomson

« C'est tout à l'honneur de Brando de s'être toujours efforcé d'avoir l'air vrai à l'écran, sans le vernis de la beauté ni de la renommée. »
David Thomson

STILL FROM 'THE CHASE' (1966)
Defending an escaped convict (Robert Redford, right), unjustly jailed and now threatened with a lynching. / Er verteidigt einen entflohenen Strafgefangenen (Robert Redford, rechts), der zu Unrecht verurteilt wurde und nun gelyncht werden soll. / Brando défendant un prisonnier en cavale (Robert Redford, à droite), injustement condamné et menacé de lynchage.

STILL FROM 'THE APPALOOSA' (1966)
Brando's career was in a long siump at this time, yet this is an excellent film. / Brandos Karriere hatte zu diesem Zeitpunkt einen langanhaltenden Tiefpunkt erreicht, doch dieser Film war herausragend. / Un excellent film tourné lors d'une longue période creuse dans la carrière de Brando.

STILL FROM 'THE APPALOOSA' (1966)
John Saxon (right) as Chuy Medina, disputes Brando (left) over a horse. / John Saxon (rechts) als Chuy Medina streitet mit Matt (Brando, links) über ein Pferd. / John Saxon (à droite), alias Chuy Medina, dans une lutte sans merci pour un cheval volé.

STILL FROM 'THE APPALOOSA' (1966)
Having survived their first encounter, Matt (Brando) again confronts Chuy (John Saxon). / Nachdem er ihre erste Begegnung überlebt hat, stellt Matt (Brando) Chuy (John Saxon) nochmals zur Rede. / Ayant survécu à leur première rencontre, Matt (Brando) affronte de nouveau Chuy (John Saxon).

STILL FROM 'THE APPALOOSA' (1966)
"The men I killed needed killin', and the women I sinned wanted sinnin', and well, I was never one much to argue." / „Die Männer, die ich getötet habe, hatten es verdient, und die Frauen, mit denen ich gesündigt habe, hatten es gewollt, und, na ja, ich hab mich noch nie auf lange Diskussionen eingelassen." / « Les hommes que j'ai tués devaient être tués, les femmes avec qui j'ai péché voulaient pécher, et moi, je suis pas du genre à discuter. »

ON THE SET OF 'A COUNTESS FROM HONG KONG' (1967)
Under the direction of Charlie Chaplin
(in foreground). / Unter der Regie von Charlie Chaplin
(im Vordergrund). / Sous la direction de Charlie Chaplin
(au premier plan).

ON THE SET OF 'A COUNTESS FROM HONG KONG' (1967)
Alas, the premise was dated, and Chaplin (standing) over-directed Brando (seated). / Die Grundidee war leider etwas angestaubt, und Chaplin (stehend) übertrieb seine Regie bei Brando (sitzend). / Hélas, l'intrigue est poussiéreuse et Chaplin (debout) dirige trop Brando (assis).

STILL FROM 'A COUNTESS FROM HONG KONG' (1967)
Playing American politician, Ogden Mears, who sails a cruise ship in an age of jet travel. / In der Rolle des amerikanischen Politikers Ogden Mears, der im Düsenzeitalter noch mit dem Kreuzfahrtschiff reist. / Dans le rôle du diplomate américain Ogden Mears, qui voyage en navire de croisière à l'ère de l'avion à réaction.

STILL FROM 'A COUNTESS FROM HONG KONG' (1967)
Chaplin insisted Brando watch him perform a scene, first, then imitate it. Here is a sample result. / Chaplin bestand darauf, dass ihm Brando zuerst zuschaute, wie er eine Szene spielte, und ihn dann nachahmte. Hier ein Beispiel für das, was dabei herauskam. / Chaplin insiste pour que Brando le regarde jouer la scène avant de l'imiter. Voici le résultat.

ON THE SET OF 'A COUNTESS FROM HONG KONG' (1967)
Chaplin (right) appears to fume impatience, winning a smile from Brando (left) and a giggle from Loren (center). / Chaplin (rechts) scheint vor Ungeduld überzuschäumen, was ihm ein Lächeln von Brando (links) und ein Kichern von Loren (Mitte) einbringt. / Chaplin (à droite) semble bouillir d'impatience, ce qui fait sourire Brando (à gauche) et glousser Sophia Loren (au centre).

STILL FROM 'A COUNTESS FROM HONG KONG' (1967)
Sophia Loren (left) as Natascha, a Russian Countess turned Hong Kong taxi-dancer. / Sophia Loren (links) als Natascha, eine russische Gräfin, die in Hongkong zum Taxigirl wird. / Sophia Loren est Natascha, une comtesse russe devenue taxi-girl à Hong Kong.

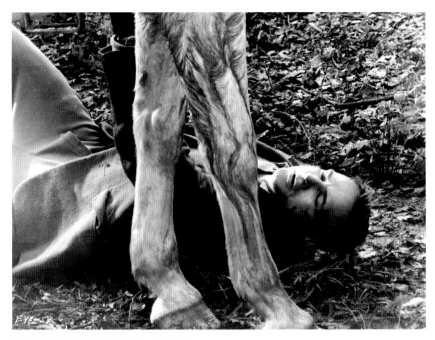

STILL FROM 'REFLECTIONS IN A GOLDEN EYE' (1967)
As Weldon Pendleton, a military man sneered at by his wife and colleagues, and even by his horse. / Als Weldon Pendleton, ein Soldat, der von seiner Frau und seinen Kollegen – und sogar von seinem Pferd – bespöttelt wird. / Dans le rôle de Weldon Pendleton, un militaire méprisé par sa femme, ses collègues et même son cheval.

ON THE SET OF 'REFLECTIONS IN A GOLDEN EYE' (1967)
The theme of a repressed homosexual in a masculine environment was daring, then, and Brando embraced the challenge. Director John Huston is crouching. / Das Thema eines heimlichen Homosexuellen in einem maskulinen Umfeld war damals gewagt, und Brando nahm die Herausforderung gerne an. Regisseur John Huston ist hockend zu sehen. / Sous la direction de John Huston (accroupi), Brando n'hésite pas à aborder un thème osé pour l'époque, celui de l'homosexualité refoulée dans un univers masculin.

"[Malcolm X] was a dynamic person, a very special human being who might have caused a revolution. He had to be done away with. The American government couldn't let him live. If 23 million blacks found a charismatic leader like he was, they would have followed him. The powers that be couldn't accept that."
Marlon Brando

„[Malcolm X] war eine dynamische Person, ein sehr besonderer Mensch, der eine Revolution ausgelöst haben könnte. Er musste ausgeschaltet werden. Die amerikanische Regierung konnte ihn nicht am Leben lassen. Wenn 23 Millionen 'Schwarze' einen charismatischen Führer wie ihn fänden, wären sie ihm gefolgt. Das konnten diejenigen, die an der Macht waren, nicht hinnehmen."
Marlon Brando

STILL FROM 'CANDY' (1968)
Brando's wild but too brief cameo as a guru remains the only reason to see this film. / Brandos wilder, jedoch allzu kurzer Cameo-Auftritt als Guru ist noch immer der einzige Grund, sich diesen Film anzutun. / L'apparition délirante mais trop brève de Brando en gourou demeure la seule raison de voir ce film.

« [Malcolm X] était un personnage dynamique, un être à part qui aurait pu provoquer une révolution. Il fallait l'éliminer. Le gouvernement américain ne pouvait pas le laisser en vie. Si 23 millions de Noirs avaient trouvé un leader aussi charismatique que lui, ils l'auraient suivi. Le pouvoir ne pouvait accepter cela. »
Marlon Brando

STILL FROM 'THE NIGHT OF THE FOLLOWING DAY' (1969)
A complex thriller about a kidnapping, with Richard Boone (top), Pamela Franklin (center), Rita Moreno (right) and Brando as an enigmatic chauffeur (front). / Ein komplexer Thriller über eine Entführung, mit Richard Boone (oben), Pamela Franklin (Mitte), Rita Moreno (rechts) und Brando als rätselhaftem Chauffeur (vorn). / Un thriller complexe autour d'un kidnapping, avec Richard Boone (en haut), Pamela Franklin (au centre), Rita Moreno (à droite) et Brando en chauffeur énigmatique (devant).

PORTRAIT FOR 'THE NIGHT OF THE FOLLOWING DAY' (1969)
Age 44, still lean and muscular. / Im Alter von 44 Jahren, noch immer schlank und muskulös. / À 44 ans, toujours mince et musclé.

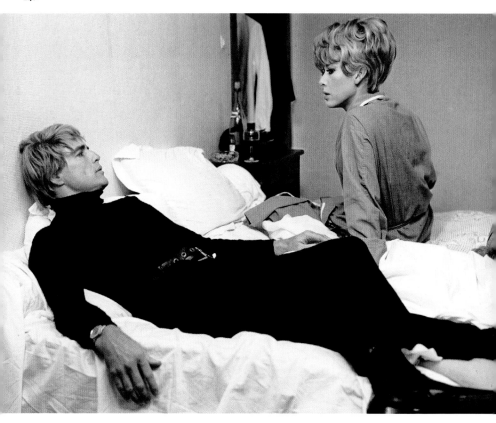

STILL FROM 'THE NIGHT OF THE FOLLOWING DAY' (1969)
"Bud," Brando's boyhood nickname, is also the name of this chauffeur, sharing a quiet moment here with Rita Moreno (right). / „Bud", Brandos Spitzname aus seiner Jugend, ist auch der Name dieses Chauffeurs, der hier einen stillen Augenblick mit Rita Moreno (rechts) teilt. / « Bud », le surnom de Brando dans son enfance, est également le nom du chauffeur, qui partage un moment d'intimité avec Rita Moreno.

"That script made about as much sense as a monkey fucking a coconut."
Marlon Brando, repenting 'Night of the Following Day' (1969)

„Das Drehbuch ergab ungefähr so viel Sinn wie ein Affe, der eine Kokosnuss vögelt."
Marlon Brando über den Film *Am Abend des folgenden Tages* (1969), den er bereute

« Ce scénario tenait à peu près autant debout qu'un singe baisant une noix de coco. »
Marlon Brando, se repentant de *La Nuit du lendemain* (1969)

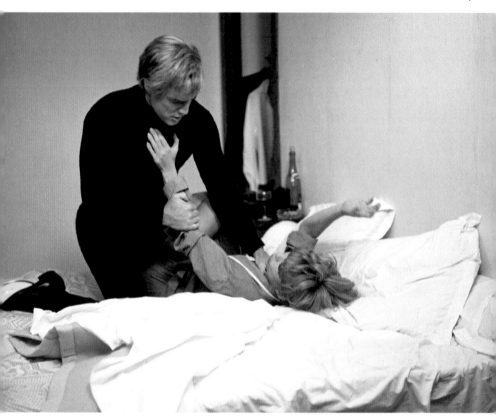

STILL FROM 'THE NIGHT OF THE FOLLOWING DAY' (1969)
Their alliance in this kidnapping also contains seeds of a fatal power struggle. / Ihre Komplizenschaft in dieser Entführung enthält auch den Keim eines tödlichen Machtkampfs. / Leur complicité lors du kidnapping contient en germe une terrible lutte de pouvoir.

PAGES 142/143
ON THE SET OF 'THE NIGHT OF THE FOLLOWING DAY' (1969)
Studying his lines – or should we say, checking out his cue cards? / Beim Lernen seines Textes – oder sollte man vielleicht besser sagen: „Beim Durcharbeiten seiner Stichworte"? / En train d'étudier ses répliques ou de vérifier ses antisèches ?

STILL FROM 'QUEIMADA' ('BURN!', 1969)
As William Walker, a suave spy working in Queimada for
the European sugar companies. / Als William Walker, ein
aalglatter Spion, der in Queimada für die europäischen
Zuckerfirmen arbeitet. / William Walker, espion
doucereux travaillant à Queimada pour le compte des
producteurs de sucre européens.

STILL FROM 'QUEIMADA' ('BURN!', 1969)
His goal is to foment a 'false revolution,' whose leaders
can be subtly controlled. / Sein Ziel ist es, eine „falsche
Revolution" anzustacheln, deren Anführer sich aus dem
Hintergrund steuern lassen. / Son but : fomenter une
fausse révolution dont les leaders pourront être
subtilement manipulés.

MOODS

LAUNEN

HUMEURS

STILL FROM 'THE NIGHTCOMERS' (1971)
These are the parts Henry James merely implied in his
classic tale, 'The Turn of the Screw.' / Dies sind die Teile,
die Henry James in seiner klassischen Novelle
Die Daumenschraube nur andeutete. / Des scènes
seulement suggérées dans le fameux roman de Henry
James, *Le Tour d'écrou.*

PAGE 146
STILL FROM 'THE NIGHTCOMERS' (1971)
As the renegade gardener, Peter Quint, opposite
Stephanie Beacham as the Nanny, Miss Jessel. / Als
abtrünniger Gärtner Peter Quint, neben Stephanie
Beacham als Kindermädchen Miss Jessel. / Le jardinier
rebelle Peter Quint, avec Stephanie Beacham dans le
rôle de la gouvernante, Miss Jessel.

*"It is a simple fact that all of us use the techniques
of acting to achieve whatever ends we seek...
Acting serves as the quintessential social lubricant
and a device for protecting our interests and
gaining advantage in every aspect of life."*
Marlon Brando

STILL FROM 'THE NIGHTCOMERS' (1971)
The relationship between the gardener and his mistress
quickly becomes sadomasochistic. / Die Beziehung
zwischen dem Gärtner und seiner Geliebten wird rasch
sadomasochistisch. / La relation entre le jardinier et
sa maîtresse tourne rapidement au sadomasochisme.

„Es ist eine einfache Tatsache, dass jeder von uns
Schauspieltechniken anwendet, um irgendein Ziel
zu erreichen, das man anstrebt ... Schauspielerei ist
das gesellschaftliche Schmiermittel schlechthin
und auch ein Mittel, unsere Interessen zu schützen
und in jedem Bereich des Lebens einen Vorteil zu
ergattern."
Marlon Brando

« C'est un fait, nous utilisons tous des techniques
de comédien pour obtenir ce que nous voulons...
Jouer la comédie est le lubrifiant social par
excellence, c'est un moyen de protéger nos intérêts
et de prendre l'avantage dans tous les domaines
de la vie. »
Marlon Brando

STILL FROM 'LAST TANGO IN PARIS' (1972)
A grieving widower, Paul (Brando, foreground),
embarking on an affair with a stranger (Maria Schneider,
in window). / Der trauernde Witwer Paul (Brando, im
Vordergrund) lässt sich auf eine Affäre mit einer
Fremden (Maria Schneider, im Fenster) ein. / Accablé
par la mort de sa femme, Paul entame une liaison avec
une inconnue (Maria Schneider, à la fenêtre).

"When Brando improvises within Bertolucci's
structure, his full art is realized."
Pauline Kael, reviewing 'Last Tango in Paris'

„Wenn Brando innerhalb des von Bertolucci
vorgegebenen Rahmens improvisiert, realisiert er
seine Kunst in vollem Umfang."
Pauline Kael in ihrer Filmkritik zu *Der letzte Tango in Paris*

« Quand Brando improvise dans le cadre établi par
Bertolucci, il atteint le sommet de son art. »
Pauline Kael dans sa critique du *Dernier Tango à Paris*

STILL FROM 'LAST TANGO IN PARIS' (1972)
Cheering himself, and feeding his demonic spontaneity,
with the gift of a dead rat to his new love. / Er muntert
sich selbst auf und nährt seine dämonische Spontaneität, indem er seiner neuen Liebe eine tote Ratte
schenkt. / Retrouvant le sourire et sa spontanéité
démoniaque en offrant un rat mort à sa nouvelle
conquête.

PAGES 152/153
STILL FROM 'LAST TANGO IN PARIS' (1972)
With his dead wife, a suicide: "You are your mother's
masterpiece." / Mit seiner Frau, die sich selbst das
Leben nahm: „Du bist das Meisterstück deiner
Mutter." / Au chevet de sa femme après son suicide :
« Tu es le chef-d'œuvre de ta mère. »

ON THE SET OF 'LAST TANGO IN PARIS' (1972)
Preparing to howl at God. Director Bernardo
Bertolucci (right) readies the shot. / Er bereitet sich
darauf vor, Gott anzuheulen. Regisseur Bernardo
Bertolucci (rechts) bereitet die Einstellung vor. /

Se préparant à haranguer Dieu. Le cinéaste
Bernardo Bertolucci (à droite) prépare le tournage.

"This may be the most powerfully erotic movie ever made... Bertolucci and Brando have altered the face of an art form."
Pauline Kael, reviewing 'Last Tango in Paris'

„Dies ist vielleicht der stärkste Erotikfilm aller Zeiten ... Bertolucci und Brando haben das Aussehen einer Kunstform verändert."
Pauline Kael in ihrer Filmkritik zu *Der letzte Tango in Paris*

« *C'est peut-être le film le plus puissamment érotique de l'histoire... Bertolucci et Brando ont changé la face du septième art.* »
Pauline Kael dans sa critique du *Dernier Tango à Paris*

STILLS FROM 'LAST TANGO IN PARIS' (1972)
Games with bodies and butter which leave both lovers utterly spent. / Spielchen mit Körpern und Butter, die beide Liebenden völlig auslaugen. / Des jeux érotiques, un peu de beurre, et les deux amants se retrouvent totalement vidés.

"We're going to make him an offer he can't refuse."
Don Vito Corleone, 'The Godfather'

„Wir werden ihm ein Angebot machen, das er nicht ausschlagen kann."
Don Vito Corleone, *Der Pate*

« Nous allons lui faire une offre qu'il ne peut refuser. »
Don Vito Corleone, *Le Parrain*

ON THE SET OF 'THE GODFATHER' (1972)
Francis Ford Coppola (right) fought hard to cast Brando
in the coveted role of mob boss Vito Corleone. / Francis
Ford Coppola (rechts) kämpfte hart darum, die
begehrte Rolle des Mafiabosses Vito Corleone mit
Brando zu besetzen. / Francis Ford Coppola (à droite) a
fait des pieds et des mains pour confier à Brando le rôle
très convoité du parrain de la Mafia, Vito Corleone.

STILL FROM 'THE GODFATHER' (1972)
The world, led by a whisper. Author Mario Puzo wrote
the novel with Marlon Brando in mind. / Die Welt, von
einem Flüstern beherrscht. Autor Mario Puzo hatte
Marlon Brando im Sinn, als er den Roman schrieb. /
Un murmure suffit à changer le monde. L'auteur Mario
Puzo a écrit le roman en pensant à Brando.

STILL FROM 'THE GODFATHER' (1972)
Mourning the death of his reckless elder son, Santino
(James Caan). / Der Pate trauert um seinen
leichtsinnigen älteren Sohn Santino (James Caan). /
Pleurant la mort de son fils aîné, Santino (James Caan).

STILL FROM 'THE GODFATHER' (1972)
Conferring his dark power on his brilliant youngest son,
Michael (Al Pacino). / Er gibt seine finstere Macht an
seinen aufgeweckten jüngsten Sohn Michael (Al Pacino)
weiter. / Confiant ses terribles pouvoirs à son fils cadet,
Michael (Al Pacino).

STILL FROM 'THE GODFATHER' (1972)
Puzo and Coppola shrewdly open their story with a
wedding: Brando, as Vito, dances with his daughter the
bride (Talia Shire). / Puzo und Coppola beginnen ihre
Erzählung klugerweise mit einer Hochzeit: Brando tanzt
als Vito mit seiner Tochter, der Braut (Talia Shire). /
Puzo et Coppola commencent judicieusement l'histoire
par un mariage : Vito (Marlon Brando) danse avec sa
fille Connie (Talia Shire).

„Ich lernte eine ganze Reihe Mafiosi kennen, und
alle erzählten mir, sie liebten den Film, weil ich den
Paten mit Würde spielte. Bis heute lassen sie mich
in Little Italy keine Rechnung zahlen.“
Marlon Brando

"I'd gotten to know quite a few Mafiosi, and all of
them told me they loved the picture because I had
played the Godfather with dignity. Even today
I can't pay a check in Little Italy."
Marlon Brando

« J'ai rencontré pas mal de mafiosi et ils m'ont tous
dit qu'ils adoraient le film parce que je jouais le
Parrain avec dignité. Aujourd'hui encore, je ne paie
jamais une addition dans le quartier italien. »
Marlon Brando

"I'm one of those people who believe that if I'm very good in this life I'll go to France when I die."
Marlon Brando

„Ich gehöre zu den Leuten, die glauben, dass sie, wenn sie in diesem Leben sehr gute Menschen sind, nach dem Tod in Frankreich landen."
Marlon Brando

« Je fais partie des gens qui croient que s'ils se comportent bien toute leur vie, ils iront en France après leur mort. »
Marlon Brando

STILL FROM 'THE GODFATHER' (1972)
Vito Corleone, having survived a lifetime of deadly attacks, now faces the prospect of a natural death. / Nachdem Vito Corleone sein Leben lang Anschläge überlebt hat, schaut er nun einem natürlichen Tod ins Auge. / Ayant survécu toute sa vie à des agressions mortelles, Vito Corleone s'apprête à mourir de mort naturelle.

PAGES 162/163
ADVERT FOR 'THE GODFATHER' (1972)
Hollywood bosses and seasoned observers were blind-sided by the magnitude of the picture's success. / Die Bosse von Hollywood waren vom ungeheuren Erfolg des Films ebenso überrascht wie langjährige Marktbeobachter. / Les magnats d'Hollywood comme les observateurs les plus aguerris sont pris de court par l'extraordinaire succès du film.

MAFIOSO MARLON MINUS HIS MUMBLE

A box-office phenomenon in America, and tipped to out-run *Gone With The Wind*, *The Godfather* opens simultaneously at four West End Cinemas this month. Shana Alexander has just completed a seven-year interview with the star, Marlon Brando.

THE Sun

THE SUN, Monday, July 31, 1972

THE MAFIA

Another great Sun...

THE SPICE OF D

He inspired the g
for years and too
the gunsmoke ha
he moved in, mo

DAY STRIKERS LOSE PLEA FOR THE DOLE

Price rise shatters home dream

THE REAL
GODFATHER

■ AS Mafia fever hits Britain with
the arrival of Marlon Brando's new
film, The Godfather, The Sun takes
a look at today's real-life Mafia—
father of their victims. The present Godfather is smiling

LUCKY

And here's
the make
believe

SENSATIONAL NA

Desperate
after years
of feuding
and failure,
he's back
slaying 'em
as a killer
with a heart

DO AS THE
GODFATHER

SUN EXCLUSIVE

STILL FROM 'THE MISSOURI BREAKS' (1976)
Writer Thomas McGuane's witty, ironic screenplay
provided a fascinating vehicle for the two stars who
then dominated Hollywood – Brando (left) and Jack
Nicholson (right). / Das geistreiche, ironische Drehbuch
von Thomas McGuane bot ein faszinierendes Vehikel
für die beiden Stars, die damals Hollywood
beherrschten: Brando (links) und Jack Nicholson
(rechts). / Le scénario mordant de Thomas McGuane
fournit un support idéal aux deux grandes stars d'alors :
Brando (à gauche) et Jack Nicholson (à droite).

STILL FROM 'THE MISSOURI BREAKS' (1976)
Next door neighbors in real life, mutual admirers Nicholson (left) and Brando only worked together on this film. / Obwohl sie sich gegenseitig bewunderten und im wahren Leben Nachbarn waren, standen Nicholson (links) und Brando nur in diesem einen Film gemeinsam vor der Kamera. / Malgré une admiration réciproque et des maisons voisines à Beverly Hills, c'est le seul film où Nicholson (à gauche) et Brando ont collaboré.

"We are all Brando's children. He gave us our freedom."
Jack Nicholson

„Wir sind alle Brandos Kinder. Er gab uns unsere Freiheit."
Jack Nicholson

« Nous sommes tous les enfants de Brando. Nous lui devons la liberté. »
Jack Nicholson

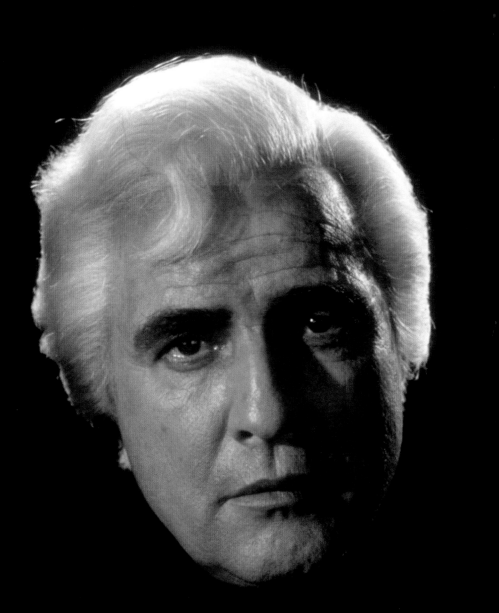

STILL FROM 'SUPERMAN' (1978)

Show me the money: Here is the first in a long line of pictures that meant little more than a payday to a great actor grown cynical. / „Zeig mal die Knete": Dies ist der erste in einer langen Reihe von Filmen, die einem inzwischen zum Zyniker gewordenen großen Schauspieler nicht mehr bedeuteten als ein dicker Scheck. / « Par ici la monnaie » : le premier d'une longue série de films purement alimentaires pour un grand acteur devenu cynique.

STILL FROM 'ROOTS: THE NEXT GENERATION' (1979)

As George Lincoln Rockwell, head of the American Nazi party, a role Brando played for scale, because he admired Alex Haley's 'Roots' saga. / Brando wurde für die Rolle des George Lincoln Rockwell, Führer der amerikanischen Nazipartei, nach Tarif bezahlt, weil er Alex Haleys Roots-Saga bewunderte. / Brando alias George Lincoln Rockwell, chef du parti nazi américain, rôle qu'il accepte par admiration pour la saga Racines d'Alex Haley.

STILL FROM 'APOCALYPSE NOW' (1979)
His last great performance, as Kurtz in this Vietnam era
update of Joseph Conrad's classic, 'Heart of
Darkness.' / Seine letzte große Rolle: als Kurtz in dieser
Übertragung von Joseph Conrads Klassiker *Herz der
Finsternis* in die Vietnam-Ära. / Son dernier grand rôle,
celui du colonel Kurtz dans un film sur la guerre du
Viêtnam librement adapté du roman de Joseph Conrad
Au cœur des ténèbres.

"You must learn to make a friend of horror."
Colonel Kurtz, 'Apocalypse Now'

*„Du musst lernen, dir die Angst zum Freund
zu machen."*
Colonel Kurtz, *Apocalypse Now*

« Il faut apprendre à apprivoiser l'horreur. »
Colonel Kurtz, *Apocalypse Now*

ON THE SET OF 'APOCALYPSE NOW' (1979)
Sorting out the complexities of this elusive role with
Francis Ford Coppola. / Mit Regisseur Francis Ford
Coppola lotet er die Komplexitäten dieser schwer
erfassbaren Rolle aus. / Brando élucide les complexités
de ce personnage insaisissable avec Francis Ford
Coppola.

STILL FROM 'THE FORMULA' (1980)
An acidly funny turn as an oil tycoon. Brando devised
this moment over breakfast, closely basing it on a photo
he'd seen of tycoon Armand Hammer. / In einer
bitterbös-witzigen Rolle als Öltycoon. Brando ließ sich
diese Szene beim Frühstück einfallen und lehnte sie eng
an ein Foto von Tycoon Armand Hammer an, das er
einmal gesehen hatte. / Portrait piquant d'un roi du
pétrole. Pour la scène du petit déjeuner, Brando s'est
inspiré d'une photo du magnat Armand Hammer.

*"People ask, 'What did you do while you took time
out?' As if the rest of my life is taking time out.
But the fact is, making movies is time out for me
because the rest, the nearly complete whole, is
what's real for me. I'm not an actor and haven't
been for years. I'm a human being - hopefully a
concerned and somewhat intelligent one - who
occasionally acts."*
Marlon Brando

STILL FROM 'A DRY WHITE SEASON' (1989)
A chance to deal with the theme of apartheid attracted Brando to this role, as barrister Ian McKenzie. / Brando gefiel die Rolle des Rechtsanwalts Ian McKenzie, weil sie ihm eine Gelegenheit bot, das Thema Apartheid zu behandeln. / Brando saisit l'occasion de traiter le thème de l'apartheid dans le rôle de l'avocat Ian McKenzie.

„Die Leute fragen: ,Was haben Sie während der Pause gemacht?' – Als ob der Rest meines Lebens Pause wäre! Tatsächlich ist das Drehen von Filmen für mich eine Pause, weil der Rest – fast der gesamte Rest – für mich Wirklichkeit ist. Ich bin kein Schauspieler und bin es schon seit Jahren nicht mehr. Ich bin ein Mensch – hoffentlich ein Mensch, der sich Gedanken macht und auch ein wenig Intelligenz besitzt – und der gelegentlich schauspielert."
Marlon Brando

« Les gens me demandent : "Que faisiez-vous quand vous preniez du temps libre ?" Comme si le reste de ma vie était un passe-temps. En réalité, c'est faire des films qui est un passe-temps pour moi, car le reste, c'est-à-dire presque toute ma vie, voilà ce qui est réel à mes yeux. Je ne suis pas acteur et ne l'ai pas été depuis des années. Je suis un être humain – un être engagé et plutôt intelligent, j'espère – à qui il arrive de faire du cinéma. »
Marlon Brando

STILL FROM 'THE FRESHMAN' (1990)
Spoofing his 'Godfather' legacy in a farce hinging on the
supposed real-life model for Vito Corleone. / In dieser
Farce über das angebliche Vorbild für Vito Corleone
macht sich Brando über sein eigenes Image als „Pate"
lustig. / Parodiant lui-même le « Parrain » dans une farce
où il est censé incarner le personnage ayant servi de
modèle à Vito Corleone.

*"Would people applaud me if I were a good
plumber?"*
Marlon Brando

*„Würden mir die Leute applaudieren, wenn ich ein
guter Klempner wäre?"*
Marlon Brando

« M'applaudirait-on si j'étais un bon plombier ? »
Marlon Brando

STILL FROM 'THE FRESHMAN' (1990)
Making his unwilling young protégé (Matthew Broderick, right) an offer he can't refuse. / Hier macht er seinem unfreiwilligen jungen Schützling (Matthew Broderick, rechts) ein Angebot, das er nicht ausschlagen kann. / Le mafioso fait à son jeune protégé (Matthew Broderick) une offre qu'il ne peut refuser.

"The only reason I'm here in Hollywood is because I don't have the moral courage to refuse the money."
Marlon Brando

„Ich bin nur aus einem einzigen Grund hier in Hollywood: weil mir die moralische Standfestigkeit fehlt, das Geld auszuschlagen."
Marlon Brando

« La seule raison pour laquelle je me trouve ici, à Hollywood, c'est que je n'ai pas le courage moral de refuser l'argent. »
Marlon Brando

STILL FROM 'DON JUAN DEMARCO' (1995)
As a psychiatrist to Johnny Depp (not pictured), finding his passion with Faye Dunaway. / Als Don Juans (Johnny Depp, nicht im Bild) Psychiater entdeckt er neue Leidenschaft für Marilyn (Faye Dunaway). / En psychiatre de Johnny Depp (absent de l'image), Brando découvre la passion avec Faye Dunaway.

STILL FROM 'CHRISTOPHER COLUMBUS: THE DISCOVERY' (1992)
A very grand inquisitor, spouting bits of pseudo-Dostoyevsky penned by Mario Puzo. Both were seeking a fat paycheck. / Ein sehr großer Großinquisitor, der mit Pseudo-Dostojewski aus der Feder von Mario Puzo um sich wirft. Sowohl Brando als auch Puzo hatten es hauptsächlich auf die fette Gage abgesehen. / En inquisiteur grandiloquent déclamant du pseudo-Dostoïevski signé Mario Puzo. Une œuvre alimentaire pour l'acteur et le scénariste.

PAGE 176, TOP/OBEN/EN HAUT
STILL FROM 'THE ISLAND OF DR. MOREAU' (1996)
Late in the day, Brando seemed to take pleasure in simply working as an actor. / Im hohen Alter schien es Brando zu gefallen, einfach nur noch als Schauspieler zu arbeiten. / À la fin de sa carrière, Brando semble prendre plaisir au simple travail d'acteur.

ABOVE/UNTEN/EN BAS
STILL FROM 'THE BRAVE' (1997)
His most soul-baring work, at the end, was accomplished under the direction of Johnny Depp (right). / Am Schluss schüttete er sein Herz aus unter der Regie von Johnny Depp (rechts). / C'est sous la direction de Johnny Depp (à droite) qu'il se mettra le plus à nu.

TOP/OBEN/EN HAUT
STILL FROM 'FREE MONEY' (1999)
Lethal farce opposite Mira Sorvino (right). / Zum
Totlachen – neben Mira Sorvino (rechts). / Aux côtés de
Mira Sorvino (à droite) dans une farce cruelle.

ABOVE/UNTEN/EN BAS
STILL FROM 'THE SCORE' (2001)
Grand, à la Sidney Greenstreet, opposite Robert De
Niro. / In großem Stil, à la Sidney Greenstreet, neben
Robert De Niro. / Une allure à la Sidney Greenstreet
aux côtés de Robert De Niro.

3

CHRONOLOGY

CHRONOLOGIE

CHRONOLOGIE

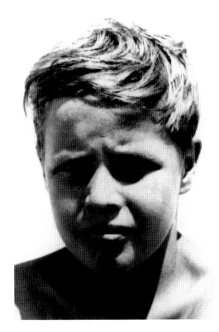

ABOVE
MARLON BRANDO (1934)

PAGE 178
MARLON BRANDO (1950)

3 April 1924 Marlon Brando, Jr. is born in Omaha, Nebraska. His father Marlon senior is a successful salesman. His artistic mother Dorothy heads the Omaha Community Players. He has two sisters: Jocelyn, who will become an actress, and Franny, who will become a visual artist.

1941 Expelled from Shattuck Military Academy at age 17 for incorrigible misbehavior. (He was caught riding a motorcycle through the school's halls.) Brando never finishes high school. A knee injury incurred while playing football for Shattuck prevents him from serving in the military.

1943 Follows his sister Jocelyn to New York, where he studies acting with Stella Adler, a protégée of the great Russian director, Konstantin Stanislavski.

19 October 1944 Brando makes his Broadway stage debut in a hit play, *I Remember Mama*.

1945 Scores an even more notable success opposite Karl Malden in Maxwell Anderson's *Truckline Café*, under the direction of Elia Kazan.

1946–1948 John Garfield and Burt Lancaster are both courted for the role of Stanley Kowalski in Tennessee Williams' *A Streetcar Named Desire*, but are either priced out of range or unavailable. Kazan, remembering how the audience couldn't take their eyes off Brando in *Truckline Café* (forcing him to adjust the blocking) suggests him for Stanley. The rest is history: the play is a smash hit with a long run, and the part is forever identified with Brando, to a degree that makes it a particular challenge for other actors to play.

1949 Goes to Hollywood to act in *The Men* (1950) for director Fred Zinnemann, and to recreate his role as Stanley Kowalski under Kazan's direction in the film version of *A Streetcar Named Desire*. In so doing, he forever trades the stage for a career in films. He will never act in a theatre again.

1950–1954 An early golden period in which Brando the screen actor cannot put a foot wrong. He turns in one perfectly realized performance after another. In 1954, he wins the Academy Award (his first) for his work in *On the Waterfront*.

1955–1960 After a battle with studio chief Darryl Zanuck over Brando's refusal to star in *The Egyptian*, the actor is obliged to accept work in a stinker (*Désirée*). And so begins the second, still high-performing but rather less ambitious era in Brando's career, in which he makes lesser pictures but becomes a box-office champion and matinee idol.

1957–1959 Marriage to his first wife, Anna Kashfi.

1961–1962 After the relative failure of his directorial debut *One-Eyed Jacks*, and after driving director Carol Reed to a headline-making nervous breakdown on *Mutiny on the Bounty* (whose budget skyrockets, and for which Brando is blamed) his career takes a comparative nose-dive.

1960–1962 Marriage to second wife, Movita.

1962–1972 Marriage to third wife, Tarita. (All in all, with and sometimes without his three wives, he will father nine children.)

1963–1971 Brando remains one of the most respected actors in the world – respected above all by other actors. For many years he stars in dud after dud (although *Bedtime Story* opposite David

Niven has its great farcical charm, and *Reflections in a Golden Eye*, directed by John Huston, demonstrates Brando still has all his talent and original voltage).

1972 *The Godfather* and *Last Tango in Paris* restore Brando to glory. The role of Vito Corleone wins him his second Oscar, which he refuses, in tribute to the civil rights struggles of American Indians. He becomes the most sought after, and priciest, actor in the world...

1973–2004 ...not to mention one of the most cynical. For the rest of his life Brando commands top fees for appearing in generally lesser pictures.

1990 Brando's Tahitian daughter Cheyenne brings her boyfriend Dag Drollet to live at the family compound atop Mulholland Drive, overlooking Hollywood. There, allegedly in the wake of a quarrel, Dag is murdered by Brando's eldest son Christian. The trial becomes a media circus. Christian is sentenced to ten years in prison and serves six.

1995 Suicide of his daughter Cheyenne, at age 25.

1 July 2004 Marlon Brando dies at age 80 in Los Angeles, of pulmonary fibrosis.

FRANCES, JOCELYN & MARLON BRANDO (1937)
His sisters were devoted to him, and vice versa. / Seine Schwestern waren ihm ergeben – und umgekehrt. / Ses sœurs et lui se vouent une grande affection.

CHRONOLOGIE

3. April 1924 Marlon Brando jr. wird in Omaha (Nebraska, USA) geboren. Sein Vater, Marlon senior, ist ein erfolgreicher Verkäufer. Seine Mutter Dorothy leitet eine Amateurtheatergruppe, die „Omaha Community Players". Marlon hat zwei Schwestern: Jocelyn, die ebenfalls Schauspielerin wird, und Franny, die bildende Künstlerin wird.

1941 Wegen unverbesserlichen Fehlverhaltens wird er im Alter von 17 Jahren von der Militärakademie Shattuck verwiesen. (Er wurde beim Motorradfahren auf den Fluren der Schule erwischt.) Brando schließt die High School nie ab. Aufgrund einer Knieverletzung, die er sich beim Footballspielen für Shattuck zugezogen hatte, ist er für den Militärdienst untauglich.

1943 Er folgt seiner Schwester Jocelyn nach New York, wo er Schauspielerei studiert unter Stella Adler, einem Schützling des großen russischen Regisseurs Konstantin Stanislawski.

19. Oktober 1944 Brando feiert sein Debüt auf der Broadway-Bühne in dem erfolgreichen Theaterstück *I Remember Mama*.

MARLON BRANDO (1950)

1945 Noch erfolgreicher ist sein Auftritt neben Karl Malden in Maxwell Andersons *Truckline Café* unter der Regie von Elia Kazan.

1946–1948 Sowohl John Garfield als auch Burt Lancaster werden umworben, die Rolle des Stanley Kowalski in Tennessee Williams' *A Streetcar Named Desire* (*Endstation Sehnsucht*) zu spielen, doch sind entweder unabkömmlich oder jenseits des Budgets. Kazan erinnert sich, wie fasziniert das Publikum von Brando in *Truckline Café* war (er musste seinetwegen sogar die Positionen der Schauspieler ändern), und schlägt ihn als Stanley vor. Der Rest ist Geschichte: Das Bühnenstück wird ein anhaltender Riesenerfolg, und die Rolle wird für alle Zeiten mit Brando in Verbindung gebracht – so sehr, dass sie für jeden anderen Schauspieler eine besondere Herausforderung darstellt.

1949 Er geht nach Hollywood, um unter der Regie von Fred Zinnemann in *The Men* (*Die Männer*, 1950) zu spielen und unter Kazans Regie seine Bühnenrolle in der Verfilmung von *A Streetcar Named Desire* (*Endstation Sehnsucht*) zu wiederholen. Damit wechselt er auch endgültig von der Bühne zum Film. Er wird nie wieder auf einer Theaterbühne stehen.

1950–1954 Eine frühe Erfolgsphase, in der Brando als Schauspieler nichts falsch machen kann: Eine vollkommene Leistung folgt der anderen. Im Jahre 1954 gewinnt er seinen ersten „Academy Award" für seine Rolle in *On the Waterfront* (*Die Faust im Nacken*).

1955–1960 Nach einer Auseinandersetzung mit dem Studioboss Darryl Zanuck über Brandos Ablehnung der Hauptrolle in *The Egyptian* (*Sinuhe der Ägypter*) muss er in der „Stinkbombe" *Désirée* (*Désirée – Napoleons erste große Liebe*) mitspielen. Damit beginnt eine zweite Phase in Brandos Karriere, in der er noch immer gute Leistungen bringt, aber sein Ehrgeiz nachlässt. Seine Filme in dieser Zeit sind eher zweitklassig, dafür aber umso erfolgreicher an den Kinokassen. Brando wird zum Schwarm der Nachmittagsvorstellungen.

1957–1959 Erste Ehe mit Anna Kashfi.

1961–1962 Mit *One-Eyed Jacks* (*Der Besessene/Noch hänge ich nicht*), seiner ersten Regiearbeit, erleidet Brando Schiffbruch, und man gibt ihm die Schuld, dass das Budget von *Mutiny on the Bounty* (*Meuterei auf der Bounty*) aus dem Ruder

läuft. Nachdem er Carol Reed, den Regisseur dieses Films, in einen schlagzeilenträchtigen Nervenzusammenbruch treibt, geht es mit seiner Karriere bergab.

1960–1962 Zweite Ehe mit Movita.

1962–1972 Dritte Ehe mit Tarita. (Insgesamt zeugt er – mit seinen drei Ehefrauen, aber auch mit anderen Frauen – neun Kinder.)

1963–1971 Brando bleibt einer der angesehensten Schauspieler der Welt – vor allem in den Augen seiner Kollegen. Seit Jahren schon spielt er in einem Flop nach dem anderen – wenngleich *Bedtime Story* (*Zwei erfolgreiche Verführer*) mit David Niven einen gewissen possenhaften Charme besitzt und Brando in *Reflections in a Golden Eye* (*Spiegelbild im goldenen Auge*) unter der Regie von John Huston beweist, dass er nichts von seinem Können und seiner ursprünglichen Kraft eingebüßt hat.

1972 *The Godfather* (*Der Pate*) und *Ultimo tango a Parigi* (*Der letzte Tango in Paris*) bringen Brandos Ruhm zurück. Für die Rolle des Don Vito Corleone erhält er seinen zweiten „Oscar", den er jedoch ablehnt, um auf den Kampf der Indianer um Bürgerrechte hinzuweisen. Er wird zum begehrtesten und teuersten Schauspieler der Welt …

UNIVERSAL STUDIOS (1956)

That is indeed Clint Eastwood standing tall at center, as Brando (seated center right) visits young actors. / Brando (sitzend in der Mitte rechts) stattet jungen Schauspielern einen Besuch ab, unter denen sich auch Clint Eastwood (hinten, Mitte) befindet. / Brando (sur un tabouret) rend visite à des acteurs en herbe, parmi lesquels le jeune Clint Eastwood (debout, au milieu).

1973–2004 … und nicht zuletzt zu einem der zynischsten. Bis zu seinem Lebensende verlangt Brando Spitzengagen für seine Auftritte in Streifen, die man meist nicht zu den Spitzenfilmen zählen kann.

1990 Brandos tahitische Tochter Cheyenne bringt ihren Freund Dag Drollet mit auf den Familienbesitz oberhalb des Mulholland Drive in Los Angeles, mit Blick auf Hollywood. Angeblich bei einem Streit wird Dag von Brandos ältestem Sohn Christian ermordet. Der Prozess wird zum Medienzirkus. Christian wird zu zehn Jahren Haft verurteilt, von denen er sechs verbüßt.

1995 Im Alter von 25 Jahren nimmt sich Tochter Cheyenne das Leben.

1. Juli 2004 Marlon Brando stirbt im Alter von 80 Jahren in Los Angeles an Lungenfibrose.

CHRONOLOGIE

3 avril 1924 Marlon Brando Jr naît à Omaha, dans le Nebraska. Son père Marlon est représentant de commerce. Sa mère Dorothy est une artiste qui dirige la troupe de théâtre municipale. Il a deux sœurs : Jocelyn, qui deviendra également actrice, et Franny, qui s'orientera vers les arts plastiques.

1941 À 17 ans, il est renvoyé de l'école militaire de Shattuck pour mauvaise conduite. (Il a été surpris traversant l'école à moto.) Il ne terminera jamais ses études secondaires. Une blessure au genou survenue lors d'un match de football l'empêche de servir dans l'armée.

1943 Il suit sa sœur Jocelyn à New York, où il étudie l'art dramatique auprès de Stella Adler, protégée du grand metteur en scène russe Konstantin Stanislavski.

ON THE SET OF 'DÉSIRÉE' (1954)
Kidding with his pal Marilyn, dropping by in a costume of her own. / Beim Herumalbern mit Kumpel Marilyn, die im eigenen Kostüm vorbeischaut. / Trinquant avec sa vieille amie Marilyn, elle aussi en costume de scène.

19 octobre 1944 Brando fait ses débuts à Broadway dans une pièce à succès, *I Remember Mama*.

1945 Il connaît un succès encore plus marqué aux côtés de Karl Malden dans la pièce *Truckline Café* de Maxwell Anderson, mise en scène par Elia Kazan.

1946–1948 John Garfield et Burt Lancaster, tous deux courtisés pour le rôle de Stanley Kowalski dans *Un tramway nommé désir* de Tennessee Williams, s'avèrent soit hors de prix, soit déjà pris. Se souvenant de l'emprise qu'il exerçait sur le public dans *Truckline Café*, Elia Kazan propose de faire appel à Brando. On connaît la suite : la pièce connaît un succès retentissant et le rôle est à jamais associé au nom de Brando, au point de le rendre particulièrement difficile à interpréter pour les autres acteurs.

1949 Il se rend à Hollywood pour jouer dans *C'étaient des hommes* (1950), du réalisateur Fred Zinnemann, et pour récréer le rôle de Stanley Kowalski dans l'adaptation au cinéma d'*Un tramway nommé désir*, tournée par Elia Kazan. Ce faisant, il abandonne définitivement les planches pour une carrière cinématographique.

1950–1954 Époque bénie où le jeune Brando semble incapable du moindre faux pas, enchaînant les rôles incarnés à la perfection. En 1954, il remporte son premier oscar pour *Sur les quais*.

1955–1960 Après s'être heurté à Darryl Zanuck, le patron de la Fox, pour avoir refusé de jouer dans *L'Égyptien*, l'acteur est contraint d'accepter un navet, *Désirée*. C'est ainsi que débute la seconde période de sa carrière, phase moins ambitieuse dans le choix des films, mais où il conserve ses talents d'acteur et devient un champion du box-office et l'idole des femmes.

1957–1959 Mariage avec sa première femme, Anna Kashfi.

1961–1962 Après l'échec relatif de *La Vengeance aux deux visages*, son premier film en tant que metteur en scène, et après avoir poussé à bout le réalisateur Carol Reed lors du tournage des *Révoltés du Bounty* (dont il serait la cause du budget astronomique), sa carrière pique du nez.

1960–1962 Mariage avec sa deuxième femme, Movita.

1962–1972 Mariage avec sa troisième femme, Tarita. (Il aura au total neuf enfants issus de ses relations conjugales et extraconjugales.)

1963–1971 Bien qu'il demeure l'un des acteurs les plus respectés au monde, notamment par ses pairs, Brando tourne navet sur navet pendant des années (même si *Les Séducteurs*, avec David Niven, possède un grand charme comique et *Reflets dans un œil d'or*, réalisé par John Huston, prouve que Brando n'a rien perdu de son talent ni de son énergie).

1972 *Le Parrain* et *Le Dernier Tango à Paris* le font remonter au firmament. Le rôle de Vito Corleone lui vaut un second oscar, qu'il refuse en soutien à la lutte des Indiens d'Amérique. Il devient l'acteur le plus convoité et le plus cher du monde …

1973–2004 … mais également l'un des plus cyniques. Pendant le restant de sa carrière, il exigera des cachets faramineux pour apparaître dans des films généralement médiocres.

STILL FROM 'BEDTIME STORY' (1964)
Brando always looked back fondly on the laughs he'd had, making this. / Brando erinnerte sich immer gerne an den Spaß, den er bei den Dreharbeiten zu diesem Film hatte. / Brando repensera toujours avec tendresse aux fous rires déclenchés par le tournage de cette scène.

1990 Cheyenne, sa fille tahitienne, ramène son petit ami Dag Drollet dans la propriété familiale de Mulholland Drive, au-dessus d'Hollywood. Dag est assassiné par Christian, le fils aîné de Brando, qui invoque une dispute. Le procès fait les choux gras des médias. Condamné à dix ans de prison, Christian en accomplira six.

1995 Suicide de sa fille Cheyenne, âgée de 25 ans.

1er juillet 2004 À 80 ans, Marlon Brando succombe à une fibrose pulmonaire à Los Angeles.

COLUMBIA PICTURES presents

MARLON BRANDO

On The Waterfront

AN ELIA KAZAN PRODUCTION

co starring
KARL MALDEN · **LEE J. COBB** with **ROD STEIGER** · **PAT HENNING** introducing **EVA MARIE SAI**

Produced by **SAM SPIEGEL** Screen Play by **BUDD SCHULBERG** Music by **LEONARD BERNSTEIN** Directed by **ELIA KAZAN**

4
FILMOGRAPHY

FILMOGRAFIE

FILMOGRAPHIE

The Men/Die Männer/C'étaient des hommes (1950)

A Streetcar Named Desire/Endstation Sehnsucht/
Un tramway nommé désir (1951)

Viva Zapata! (1952)

Julius Caesar/Julius Caesar/Jules César (1953)

The Wild One/Der Wilde/L'Équipée sauvage
(1954)

On the Waterfront/Die Faust im Nacken/Sur les
quais (1954)

Désirée/Désirée - Napoleons erste große
Liebe/Désirée (1954)

Guys and Dolls/Schwere Jungen, leichte
Mädchen/Blanches colombes et vilains messieurs
(1955)

The Teahouse of the August Moon/Das kleine
Teehaus/La Petite Maison de thé (1956)

Sayonara (1957)

The Young Lions/Die jungen Löwen/Le Bal des
maudits (1958)

The Fugitive Kind/Der Mann in der Schlangenhaut/
L'Homme à la peau de serpent (1960)

One-Eyed Jacks/Der Besessene (Noch hänge ich
nicht)/La Vengeance aux deux visages (1961)

Mutiny on the Bounty/Meuterei auf der Bounty/
Les Révoltés du Bounty (1962)

The Ugly American/Der häßliche Amerikaner/
Le Vilain Américain (1963)

Bedtime Story/Zwei erfolgreiche Verführer/
Les Séducteurs (1964)

Morituri (The Saboteur/Code Name: Morituri)/
Kennwort: Morituri/Morituri (1965)

The Chase/Ein Mann wird gejagt/La Poursuite
impitoyable (1966)

The Appaloosa/Südwest nach Sonora/L'Homme
de la Sierra (1966)

A Countess from Hong Kong/Die Gräfin von Hongkong/La Comtesse de Hong-Kong (1967)

Reflections in a Golden Eye/Spiegelbild im goldenen Auge/Reflets dans un œil d'or (1967)

Candy (1968)

The Night of the Following Day/Am Abend des folgenden Tages/La Nuit du lendemain (1969)

Queimada (Burn!)/Queimada – Insel des Schreckens/Queimada (1969)

The Nightcomers/Das Loch in der Tür/ Le Corrupteur (1971)

The Godfather/Der Pate/Le Parrain (1972)

Last Tango in Paris/Der letzte Tango in Paris/ Le Dernier Tango à Paris (1972)

The Missouri Breaks/Duell am Missouri/ Missouri Breaks (1976)

Superman (1978)

Apocalypse Now (1979)

The Formula/Die Formel/La Formule (1980)

A Dry White Season/Weiße Zeit der Dürre/ Une saison blanche et sèche (1989)

The Freshman/Freshman/Premiers pas dans la Mafia (1990)

Christopher Columbus: The Discovery/ Christopher Columbus: Der Entdecker/ Christophe Colomb : la découverte (1992)

Don Juan DeMarco (1995)

The Island of Dr. Moreau/D.N.A. – Experiment des Wahnsinns (DNA – Die Insel des Dr. Moreau)/L'Île du docteur Moreau (1996)

The Brave (1997)

Free Money (1999)

The Score (2001)

A Film by BERNARDO BERTOLUCCI
with MARIA SCHNEIDER · MARIA MICHI · GIOVANNA GALLETTI and with JEAN-PIERRE LEAUD starring MASSIMO GIROTTI
Produced by ALBERTO GRIMALDI Directed by BERNARDO BERTOLUCCI A COPRODUCTION PEA PRODUZIONI EUROPEE ASSOCIATE S.A.1 - ROME LES PRODUCTIONS ARTISTES ASSOCIES S.A - PARIS
United Artists
Original Motion Picture Soundtrack Available on United Artists Records and Tapes

Charles Chaplin Presents

Marlon
Brando

Sophia
Loren

BIBLIOGRAPHY

Bly, Nelly: *Marlon Brando: Larger Than Life.* Pinnacle Books, 1994.

Bosworth, Patricia: *Marlon Brando.* Phoenix, 2002.

Brando, Marlon: *Songs My Mother Taught Me.* Random House, 1994.

Brion, Patrick: *Marlon Brando.* Éditions de la Martinière, 2006.

Englund, George: *Marlon Brando. The Way It's Never Been Done Before.* Harper Perennial, 2005.

Fauser, Jörg: *Marlon Brando - Der versilberte Rebell.* Alexander Verlag, 2004.

Feldvoß, Marli & Löhndorf, Marion: *Marlon Brando.* Bertz + Fischer, 2004.

Fiore, Carlo: *Bud - The Brando I Knew.* Delacorte Press, 1974.

Kashfi-Brando, Anna, with Stein, E.P.: *Brando for Breakfast.* Crown Publishers, 1979.

Manso, Peter: *Brando, the Biography.* Hyperion, 1994.

Porter, Darwin: *Brando Unzipped.* Blood Moon Productions, 2006.

Ryan, Paul: *Marlon Brando: A Portrait.* Carroll & Graf Pub, 1994.

Schickel, Richard: *Brando.* Thunder's Mouth Press, 2000.

Schickel, Richard: *Marlon Brando: A Portrait of a Generation.* Chrysalis Books, 1990.

Schickel, Richard: *Brando: A Life in Our Times.* Atheneum, 1991.

Schirmer, Lothar: *Marlon Brando.* Schirmer, 1995.

Teriipaia, Tarita: *Marlon Brando, mon amour, ma déchirure.* Pocket, 2006.

Thomas, Tony: *The Films of Marlon Brando,* Citadel Press, 1973.

Thomson, David: *Marlon Brando.* Dorling Kindersley Publishing, 2003.

IMPRINT

© 2006 TASCHEN GmbH
Hohenzollernring 53, D-50672 Köln
www.taschen.com

Editor/Picture Research/Layout: Paul Duncan/Wordsmith Solutions
Editorial Coordination: Martin Holz, Cologne
Production Coordination: Nadia Najm and Horst Neuzner, Cologne
German translation: Thomas J. Kinne, Nauheim
French translation: Anne Le Bot, Paris
Multilingual production: www.arnaudbriand.com, Paris
Typeface Design: Sense/Net, Andy Disl and Birgit Reber, Cologne

Printed in Italy

ISBN-13: 978-3-8228-2002-5
ISBN-10: 3-8228-2002-4

To stay informed about upcoming TASCHEN titles, please request our magazine at www.taschen.com/magazine or write to TASCHEN, Hohenzollernring 53, D-50672 Cologne, Germany, contact@taschen.com, Fax: +49-221-254919. We will be happy to send you a free copy of our magazine which is filled with information about all of our books.

All the photos in this book, except for those listed below, were supplied by The Kobal Collection.

The Jim Heimann Collection: pp. 42/43